CRIMES
OF PASSION
THE DARK SIDE OF THE HEART

WHITE STAR PUBLISHERS

WS White Star Publishers® is a registered trademark
property of De Agostini Libri S.p.A.

© 2016 De Agostini Libri S.p.A.
Via G. da Verrazano, 15
28100 Novara, Italy
www.whitestar.it - www.deagostini.it

Project editor and editorial assistant: ICEIGEO, Milano (Margherita Giacosa,
Chiara Schiavano, Paola Paudice, Giulia Gatti)
Translation: Jonathan West, Canice Murray. Editing: Max Rankenburg

ISBN 978-88-544-1026-8
1 2 3 4 5 6   20 19 18 17 16

Printed in Malta

Text by: Carlo Batà, Francesco Biselli, Giulia Gatti, Francesca Gentile,
Margherita Giacosa, Federica Guarnieri, Francesca Guerrini, Lorenzo Marsili,
Roberto Mottadelli, Giorgio Oldrini, Paola Paudice, Francesca Scanzi,
Chiara Schiavano

CRIMES
OF PASSION
THE DARK SIDE OF THE HEART

EDITED BY

MARGHERITA GIACOSA AND CHIARA SCHIAVANO

Contents

Introduction

To define the limits of a "crime of passion" is anything but simple. Above all, let's resist the temptation to take the most classical of shortcuts by turning to the idea of "love". It is clear what a crime is: a grave infraction, an act that breaks the law and is thus severely punished. The concept of passion has much more nuance, but at its origin is a very strong emotion, an urge so intense that it weakens rationality and objectivity. It is thus able to create extreme conditions in which the likelihood increases that crime will be committed: a short-circuit through which violent emotion can become real violence, due to – so to speak – a partial or total absence of lucidity.

There are many thorns, more or less poisonous, on this blood-colored rose. Calumnies, threats, violations of privacy, persecution, verbal and physical aggression. Emotions and behaviors become more chronic until they reach the crime, murder, which is only rarely committed in a sudden fit of madness.

This volume brings together stories of murderers. Stories of humanity numbed by the senses and by sexual desire, by the hallucination of possession, by insecurity, by fear, by uncontrollable urges . . . And yet the irrational often transforms in such conditions into ice-cold calculations and behaviors. All taken to the most extreme consequences.

Cherchez la femme?

Alexandre Dumas *père* said it. In *Black Dahlia*, James Ellroy, another master of narrative intrigue, repeated it: *Cherchez la femme*. No matter what the crime is, whatever the apparent causes may be, deep down the reason is a woman. A woman who denies herself, whom someone is jealous of, whom someone feels abandoned by, or whom someone has been stirred up by.

If we consider literature alone, *cherchez la femme* would seem to be a maxim tailor-made for crimes of passion, from Homer to Shakespeare, from the final duet of *Cavalleria Rusticana* to the modern noir classics. This would be true if it were not for the fact that reality is so much more complex than the clichés of fiction. And even those of gender.

Because it is a fact that usually, in crimes of passion, the plot unfolds in a triangular scenario, and to each corner there corresponds a protagonist of the drama. And the action consists in the elimination of one the subjects (sometimes even two). But guilty parties, victims, and objects of desire can be interpreted by more than one protagonist, and often there is no need to search for the woman: she is already there, lifeless, at the beginning of the investigation. Maybe she's in the gutter, as in the case of the *The Girl in Yellow Pajamas*, or, more often, in the bedroom, where the husband is telling the detectives that he knows nothing (*Who Killed Marilyn Sheppard?*).

In other cases, on the other hand, identifying the woman proves to be fundamental, not in search of motive but, quite simply, in finding the guilty person. These are the cases which generally attract the most attention in the media: partly because they are less frequent, partly because they tend to bring into play less obvious categories, to upset conventional ideas, and to express horror in unpredictable ways. Perhaps by masking it in gentleness: as in the case of the French grandmother who seems to have come out of fairy tale, and yet she cuts her lover and perhaps also her husband into pieces (*A Well-respected Woman*), which is unconsciously imitated by a beautiful ice cream parlor owner in Vienna (*The Ice Cream Murderess*), who is incapable of saying goodbye to the men she has loved in any other way. Or by mixing eroticism and cruelty, giving physical form to archetypal male nightmares: just think of the geisha who, to have her man all for herself, goes so far as to kill him and emasculate him after an erotic game (*Love Takes Your Breath Away*). Or of the homosexual lovers who decide to eliminate the husband of one of them, taking revenge for years of violence inflicted by men (*In the Name of Sappho*). To the point of demolishing explicitly the two pillars of society, the family and blood ties with children: the revenge of a disappointed lover taken on the children of the legitimate wife (*The Beast of Via San Gregorio*) and, in a crescendo of disturbing madness, the mother who kills her own little girl, the perverse proof of devotion to man who has psychologically subjugated her (*The Ballad of Blind Love*).

Obviously, in the case of crimes committed by women, there are also more "linear" plots, with the golden formula of treachery-jealousy-revenge expressed in various forms. From the wife who, in league with her lover, poisons a drink for her husband (*The Gentian Bitters Crime*) to the high-society lady who, in front of her husband, shoots her ex-lover who's guilty of preferring other women (*Under the White Ermine*). All in all, while the expression "crime of passion" might offer the motive, it neither indicates the kind of victim, nor the kind of murderer.

It's the press, baby

There are not many news items that arouse mass curiosity like crimes of passion. These are crimes in which the fascination of the mystery – with its inevitable accompanying reconstructions and conjectures, suspicions and *coup de théâtre* – is augmented by morbid gossip. Sooner or later, the investigations reveal the intimate life of victims and (presumed) murderers. If the investigators do not search enough, it is the journalists who snoop above and below the sheets: the press has prospered for more than a century on blood and sex – the prosaic but effective epitome of the *liaison dangereuse* between Eros and Thanatos.

The intrusiveness of the mass media, and their inflammatory impact on public opinion, are the common elements in almost all the crimes included in this volume, which we have selected from those occurring after 1900. Already at the dawn of what would be described as "the Century of the media", court reports became "a favored instrument of the silent revolution which saw people gain access to literacy and reading", to quote the well-known French study by the historian Dominique Kalifa. This is symbolized by the sensation caused in 1902 by the Murri case (*The Charming Crime of Bologna*), which blazed not only in the Italian media, but echoed well beyond the national borders.

The crimes of passion related by the newspapers are similar to the popular serialized novels published by these same papers. It is enough to think of *The Trial of the Russians*, which in 1907 displayed the secret world of parties, drugs, and femmes fatales hidden behind highfalutin aristocratic titles, an intrigue cinematically culminating in tragedy among the canals of Venice.

Stories like this were much more interesting than the *feuilletons*. Not only because the facts described had really happened, but because attorneys and prosecutors, witnesses, experts, and the accused were allowed, or rather required, to describe acts which the common sense of decency made unutterable outside that context. And the newspapers did not fail to allude to the raciest details, on both sides of the Atlantic: in 1922 the United States was in a state of excitement because of the explicit love letters that the faithless clergyman and the wife of his sacristan had exchanged, before being murdered together (*In the Shade of the Crabapple Tree*).

Needless to say, public and media attention reach a paroxysm when the crime of passion involves well-known figures. It matters little whether they are the victims or the presumed to be guilty: from the case of the Philippine actress Lilian Vélez (*"Pop, Narding Has Killed Mom!"*) to the controversial story of the athlete Oscar Pistorius (*The Bullet in the Chamber*), by way of the case of O. J. Simpson (*An American Tragedy*). This will always remain in the collective imagination as a crime of passion, although the accused was acquitted.

The ability of the parties in the dispute to use the mass media for their own needs, both in facts and in fiction, is certainly not a negligible element. The defense of the millionaire Harry Thaw (*The Red Velvet Swing*) quickly intuited that the media could be exploited to manipulate a galvanized public opinion, which, in turn, could influence trials and discredit verdicts: during the proceedings an instant movie was produced in support of the accused. This depicted him as a paladin of the American values, showed a trial and concluded with his acquittal. Hot on its heels, there followed derivative books and films which related the facts more or less faithfully, all of which contributed to an increased confusion between the truth of the media and that of the Court. This is apart from confronting the extremely delicate theme of the relationship between judicial truth and the reality of events: many verdicts cited in this volume – including Thaw's mild punishment – are, decades later, unconvincing, and in many cases there is a widespread call to reopen trials that were quickly concluded.

In a wider context, it is not surprising that crimes of passion have fascinated many film directors, including David W. Griffith, Alfred Hitchcock, Luchino Visconti, and Miloš Forman. It is symbolic that a case for which objective reconstruction is most difficult, almost impossible, should concern the publishing magnate William Randolph Hearst – the man who is said to have inspired *Citizen Kane* by Orson Welles – and involves the gilded world of the cinema (*The Hollywood Mystery*): it is a story in which it is not even clear whether or not a crime of passion was committed. The crime was shrouded, by publishers and producers, in secrecy. Paradoxically, it was Hearst's society that then has transformed crimes of passion into spectacle.

Roberto Mottadelli

The Charming Crime of Bologna

Linda and Tullio Murri (Italy)

"If you didn't read about it in the French newspapers, you'd never believe such things could happen. Paris, dubbed the modern Babylon, capital of the world, etc., envies Bologna the Learned, the mortadella capital – but not because of its University, its tortellini, its Felsina water. No, ladies and gentlemen, Paris envies Bologna for its fine tragedy that transpired on Via Mazzini, with its dead and wounded. If you don't believe the *Rana* of Bologna, maybe you'll find *Le Figaro* of Paris more convincing: «This Italian murder – truly, a charming crime»".

There's probably a rat trapped between the doors, or maybe something terrible has happened, thinks Teresa Cicognani, the concierge of Via Mazzini 39, a handsome building which looks onto the portico of Santa Maria dei Servi. The late summer air, in the streets in the center of Bologna, is close: there is not a breath of wind. And that disgusting smell on the stairs is becoming more pungent by the hour, alarming the woman at the entrance to the respectable building. She reconciles herself to the Bonmartinis not being at home. She has almost broken down the door with her knocking. Count Francesco and his wife Linda Murri are probably still with the children at the baths at Lido di Venezia. It's necessary to tell the professor. However, Augusto Murri, a respected doctor and luminary of the University, does not have the keys to Palazzo Bisteghi, where his daughter lives. Maybe Tullio, the professor's younger child, has copies. The latter hastens there as soon as he is told, rushing from the provincial assizes on that September 2nd, 1902. A young lawyer with a passion for politics, he was elected councilor for the Socialist Party at only twenty-eight years old, defeating his opponent, the famous poet Giosuè Carducci. But Tullio neither has the keys.

In front of the main door of the apartment the stench is unbearable. While Tullio and Teresa watch the locksmith force the lock, the inspector sent by the police department covers his nose with a handkerchief. Once inside, they find the horror.

Surrounded by appalling chaos, the corpulent body of the Count lay on the floor, in a pool of congealed blood. Pierced by 13 deep wounds in the chest and face, there are worms on his neck, his carotid artery brutally severed, and a swarm of flies feeds from his nostrils. The body is in an advanced state of decay. Death took place at least six days before.

The crime scene immediately suggests an unsuccessful burglary, or a trap disguised as love date. The pockets of the Count's

---

In the middle, professor Augusto Murri with the wife Giannina; on his right, their daughter Linda and, behind her, her husband, the Count Francesco Bonmartini.

gray jacket are turned inside out, drawers and cupboards are in chaos, and the Countess's jewels have disappeared. On the table there is a bottle of champagne and two glasses, there is a pair of pink panties in the unmade bed, and there is long hair in the wash-basin. A note found in the Count's wallet mentions a romantic *rendez-vous* with a woman who signs only with the letter B. There is no trace of the murder weapon.

Inside the Palazzo Bisteghi

The inspector came to quick conclusions. It was no mystery that the victim had had extramarital affairs, courted and associated

IN THE NEWSPAPER SERIES

The newspapers were late in giving the news of Count Bonmartini's death: nothing was published until September 3rd. However, the events of Via Mazzini rapidly seized everyone's attention. The first interesting aspect was the figures involved: a rich middle-class family, professional people who were involved in the public life of the city but who had turbulent private lives. The elements for a front-page story gradually appeared.
At the beginning of the century, public opinion was attracted by court cases; the proceedings of the Courts quickly became the "favored means for a silent revolution in which the people gained access to literacy and to reading". The true stories resembled the *feuilletons* published in installments in the newspapers. Moreover, they were more interesting, because the events were garnished with risqué, clever details. The journalists discovered them by improving their investigative methods, and organizing parallel investigations to those of the police. With the Murri case, newspaper sales soared, and some newspapers even succeeded in printing three daily editions to satisfy the readers and keep up with the *coups de théâtre*. It was the first great demonstration of press power.

with young singers and women in show business. It was a simple consequence of his lack of foresight that one of them had played a dirty trick on him. Francesco Bonmartini, thirty-three years old, was an honest but mediocre man who was not particularly smart or gifted. His noble Paduan origins had a guaranteed him a good marriage and the hope of a position as assistant to professor Murri. However, this position had never materialized. After the first two months of passionate love, the differences between Linda and Francesco had come to dominate. Easy affairs had took up the Count's free time, as he could hardly bear his wife's coldness. After an attempt at reconciliation signed before Cardinal Svampa through the efforts of Tullio, for whom his sister's happiness was all-important, the fighting began again, worse than before. Their separation was a fact.

The city expressed its condolences to the Murri family, stricken both by grief and by shame. However, there were many details in the events and in the motive which puzzled both detectives and the press. They slowly began to formulate theories and questions. What if the crime scene had been prepared to mislead the investigators? Who had a motive to eliminate the Count?

Coups de Théâtre

They soon slapped the monster on page one: on September 12th, only two days after the funeral, Tullio Murri was arrested. In a confession written in Ulm, where in the meantime he had taken refuge, and which was given to his father, he told of a necessary gesture of self-defense. The file was delivered spontaneously by Augusto Murri himself to judge Stanzani, who was in charge of the investigation, a dramatic gesture which upset mood and public order.

Tullio's reconstruction began from an attempt to clear the air between the two. Bonmartini had threated moving back to Padua with the children, leaving a city that had always considered him a foreigner. Tullio, knowing his sister's delicate state of health and her love for her children, had asked him to reconsider his decision. On another occasion, Tullio wrote to a friend:

> *It is an inexpressible torture to see my poor sister so miserable, unfortunate and suffering, without being able to help her! I love her immensely (…). If I could impute to someone the ills afflicting her, I'd become a criminal before nightfall.*

Soon the discussion he requested had turned into a passionate argument. Bonmartini had offended the sister's dignity and her father's honor, provoking outbreaks of rage in Murri. Then the Count had drawn a knife. A furious struggle to the last breath ensued, in which Tullio, who was impulsive and determined, got the better of the Count.

Political Battles

On the basis of these facts, the city split into two factions in an instant. He might be a ladies' man, but the count was still a Christian noble. *L'Avvenire d'Italia*, the standard bearer of the clerical press, defended him and raised him to the status of martyr. The Murri family, on the contrary, had a different, socialist and anticlerical, background. In particular, Tullio, who described himself as a free thinker and a positivist, who lived a Bohemian life (even more than his brother-in-law) was supported by *Avanti!*

and *Il Resto del Carlino*. In any case, the suspicion remained that there was a still deeper truth, that the confession was aimed at protecting someone, perhaps his sister Linda – there was nasty gossip about their relationship, whispers of incest – or even the father, however upright he appeared to all.

Just two days went by and Linda, too, was arrested, accused of being the brain behind the murder, her brother's instigator and accomplice. Her affair with Carlo Secchi, twenty years older than she was, broke into the news. They had been in love when they were young. They had stifled their passion, which had re-awakened when her marriage went into a crisis, and often consumed it in the *pied-à-terre* in the same building, the entrance of which looked onto a quieter street, Vicolo Posterla.

At this point, the struggle became social and the crime an excuse for a political campaign: the Socialists, on one side, argued that the institution of divorce was an effective means to avoid crimes of passion; the clericals, on the other hand, condemned the absence of morality, blaming the lapse into licentiousness which "forces Man toward violence, dulling the intellect after having ruined his heart".

There was a chain of other arrests: besides Carlo Secchi, Pio Naldi, a pupil of the Professor's and friend of Tullio's; Rosa Bonetti, a nurse and lover of Tullio's, and finally Ernesto and Severo Dalla, servants in the Murris' home, who were then released. After all the protagonists had been identified, the picture became clear.

First-degree murder. Carlo had supplied the curare, a powerful poison, for other unsuccessful attempts. Tullio, with the complicity of Pio, had waited for the Count to come home. Together they had killed him, and then with the help of Rosa and the blessing of Linda they had created the scene which should have thrown the investigators off the scent.

Only now did the individuals involved in the affair realize that they had simply been minor players, directed by Linda and Tullio Murri.

Large Numbers

Beginning on October 11th, 1904, the date assigned for the first hearing – which was immediately postponed to February 21st and transferred to Turin (where there were less involved) – there followed 104 hearings in which 420 witnesses appeared. Every time it was a little show. A model of the Palazzo Bisteghi was constructed, even with a removable roof, and knives were used equipped with a dynamometer to measure the force required to stave in a man's breastbone.

On August 11th, 1905, the sentences were given before an uncontainable crowd, both inside and outside the courtroom: 30 years for Tullio and Pio Naldi, guilty of murder with the aggravating circumstance of premeditation; 10 years for Linda and Carlo Secchi, found guilty of being an "accessory after the fact"; 7 years and 6 months for Rosa Bonetti, also an accessory, whose partial mental infirmity was recognized. They all appealed, but without success.

Only Linda was pardoned after a year in prison by King Vittorio Emanuele III, a gesture of gratitude to professor Augusto Murri, who had saved his daughter, the princess, from a certain death.

The Red Velvet Swing

Stanford White (United States)

A young girl of legendary beauty, a famous but sexually unscrupulous architect and a multimillionaire with mental problems were the key characters in what the American press called "the crime of the century". The background is New York at the beginning of the 20th Century, a society caught between the after-effects of Victorian puritanism and the excesses of the *nouveau riche*.

Florence Evelyn Nesbit arrived in New York with her mother in 1900. Her father, an unambitious lawyer without much business sense, had died a few years before, leaving her mother Florence, younger brother Howard and herself penniless. At fourteen, Evelyn found herself forced to work as a store clerk in a department store in Philadelphia, where the family had moved from Pittsburgh. Her classical looks were noticed by a local painter, and she began to work as a model with the blessing of her mother, who was swayed by the pay of a dollar a day and reassured by the fact that Evelyn would be working for a woman artist.

The girl quickly became the favorite model of Philadelphia's illustrators, painters and artists, and soon earned more in a few days than a store clerk was paid in a month. When she decided to move to New York to look for work, her mother went with her and took a sheaf of letters of recommendation written by her artist patrons. From being a model out of necessity, she soon became the muse of choice of the New York artistic community. Her portraits were published in the leading magazines of the day

Harry Thaw behind bars for the murder of the architect Stanford White.
In the next page: Stanford White and Florence Evelyn Nesbit.

such as *Harper's Bazaar*, *Cover Girl*, and *Vanity Fair*. Her direct, intense look became the feminine face of the turn of the century: Evelyn Nesbit was the first top model.

Intelligent and hungry for new experience, she convinced her mother to accompany her to auditions for new musical comedies being staged on Broadway. The theater industry was booming in New York, and Evelyn was soon cast as a chorus-line dancer in the *Florodora* show at the Casino Theatre on 39th Street. It was there that she met the man who would change all their lives: Stanford White, one the most successful, scintillating and creative architects in New York, was particularly uninhibited in flaunting his wealth. His friends were bankers, financiers, actors and artists.

The Room with Mirror Walls

Stanford White first met Evelyn after a theater show in 1902. He was 47, she was 16. Part Pygmalion, part benefactor, he moved Evelyn and her family into a new, sumptuously decorated apartment. He showered the girl with expensive gifts and introduced her to the most exclusive circles, making her a true celebrity. He guaranteed an income for her mother (who was finally released from her dire economic straits) and used his influence to get young Howard a place in the Military Academy.

The first time that Evelyn entered the architect's house on 24th Street, he invited her to play a game on a red velvet swing in a room on the second floor. In the presence of a couple of his friends, she had to swing up to a paper parasol on the ceiling and kick it to pieces. Nothing more happened that day. Evelyn returned home and told her mother how much she had been amused.

After some months, White paid for Evelyn's mother to return to Pittsburgh to visit relatives and invited the girl up to his downtown apartment again. Afterwards, she claimed she had entered a room with mirror walls:

... a virgin, but didn't come out as one.

After her relationship with White, which lasted a little more than a year, Evelyn had other relationships, the most important of which was with John Barrymore, an actor and lover of the good

FIRST TOP MODEL

Once Evelyn arrived in New York her success was fast. In a few months her face was reproduced on calendars and postcards, and helped to sell such products as skin creams and tooth-paste. She was the muse and inspiration of famous works of art such as the statue *Innocence* by George Grey Barnard and the drawing by Charles Dana Gibson entitled *Woman: The Eternal Question*, where her perfect profile is framed by a question mark formed by her hair.

life. White didn't approve of the relationship, and persuaded her mother to enroll Evelyn in a boarding school for girls in New Jersey. A few months after this, the girl was taken to the hospital: officially for an appendicitis operation, it was widely believed that she had an abortion. The hospital expenses were paid by Harry Thaw, a multimillionaire from Pittsburgh who had been courting Evelyn for a long time. Harry had suffered from mental problems since infancy and was a cocaine addict who frequented New York's high society. After the operation, he arranged for Evelyn and her mother to take a tour of Europe with him.

Horror and Marriage

All three visited London and Paris, and then her mother returned to New York leaving the young couple by themselves. During the late stages of the tour Harry became ever more disturbed and began to develop an obsession about White: he questioned Evelyn continually on the nature of her relationship with the architect.

One night, while they were in a castle in the Austrian Alps, she confessed to the violence she had endured in the room with the mirror walls. Harry Thaw was transformed into a monster. In a psychotic fit he tied her up, held her prisoner for two weeks, whipped and raped her. Following on this horror came apologies, tears and a proposal of marriage. Evelyn was persuaded: they were married on April 4th, 1905, and went to live in the Thaw family residence in Pennsylvania.

It was not a happy period. Harry became increasingly obsessed with hatred for White and made it the aim of his life to unmask the transgressions of the architect.

Married to Bessie Springs Smith, the heiress of a Long Island family, Stanford White was notorious for his extramarital affairs with young girls. Besides his family house a few kilometers from Manhattan on the Golden Coast of Long Island, White had restructured a mansion on 24th Street: it was a place of parties and secret encounters, where friends, young girls, potential clients and rich New Yorkers came in search of certain experiences. White had a red velvet swing installed in one of the larger rooms on the second floor of the building, and had a bedroom beside it fitted with mirror walls.

On the evening of June 25th, 1906, Harry and Evelyn attended a play on the roof of Madison Square Garden, designed and built by Stanford White. Towards the end of the evening the architect himself appeared and was shown to his reserved table. Harry Thaw and Evelyn rose to leave a little later. Unexpectedly, the man retraced his steps, stopped in front of White, pulled out a pistol and shot him three times. Then he held the gun aloft and shouted:

I killed him because he ruined my wife!

Without Remorse

When the trial opened, it had all the elements to make it the focus of public curiosity: wealth, desire, passion, madness, vengeance. The twenty-eight New York daily papers of the day reported every detail of the trial and transformed the judicial case into a media event. Harry Thaw's mother paid out millions of dollars in legal expenses to defend her son, who risked capital punishment. The defensive strategy was simple but effective: to present the accused as the protector of Evelyn's virtue and to

A FILM TO INFLUENCE THE PUBLIC

During the trial, the Thaw family produced a 12-minute film entitled *The Unwritten Law* and distributed it round New York cinemas. The film reconstructs the Evelyn, White and Thaw Affair. The crime committed by Thaw is presented as an action to defend the dignity of his wife, and the film concludes with the acquittal of the defendant. *The Unwritten Law* was only the first of a number of films based on the case; among the more well known are *The Girl in the Red Velvet Swing* of Richard Fleischer (1955), in which the part of Evelyn Nesbit was played by Joan Collins, and *Ragtime* (1981), a film of Miloš Forman in which Elizabeth McGovern had the part of Evelyn.

demonize the victim as a monster without moral values who corrupted young girls. At the same time, the lawyers played the mental illness card by inventing an "American dementia", a form of madness characterized by an unrestrainable impulse of husbands to save the honor of their wives.

The jury in the first trial, which lasted three months, could not agree on a verdict. At the end of the second trial, however, Harry Thaw was found guilty but insane and sentenced to detention in a psychiatric hospital. Evelyn Nesbit testified in both cases; she readily described her abuse by White at sixteen years old but, reportedly in exchange for a promise of divorce and a considerable sum of money, was much more reticent in describing the repeated violence inflicted by her husband.

After various incidents, including his escape from the asylum, Harry was declared a free man in 1915. But the violence did not stop: he underwent a new trial the following year for kidnapping and sexually assaulting a boy. Sentenced for the second time, he was released in 1924, and died aged seventy-six in Florida, without ever repenting the crimes he had committed.

On the Eve
of the Wedding

Grete Beier (Germany)

The bell tolls heavily in the first light of dawn on July 23rd, 1908. It is the signal for the condemned woman to enter. She appears to be untroubled, with her back straight and an unwavering gaze. Twenty-two years old, in a black dress, Grete Beier is without fear. She leads the way, before her defense attorney and a gentle Protestant pastor, her confessor, who follow her up the five steps of the gallows in the courtyard of Freiburg Prison, in Saxony.

No gesture, no tremor, no veiled grimace while she confronts the gaze of those assembled for the macabre spectacle. Before her eyes there are 190 men in uniforms of the Prefecture, complete with top hats. They are all immaculately dressed, as has been requested. The woman's wrists and ankles are secured to the wooden pole with great straps, and her neck is held in two semicircular supports. Only then does she lose control and cry:

Father, into Thy hands I commit my spirit! Father, into Thy hands …

The executioner releases the rope and the blade of the guillotine drops down on her. Her head falls into the basket. The spectacle lasts no more than three minutes.

An Angelic Face, Intelligent and Well-off

In the papers and in the street people talked for a long time about Grete Beier, the daughter of the mayor and chief of police of Brand, a small town in Saxony. Flowers were laid for weeks on her grave, placed next to that of her father, who died of a broken heart when she was arrested. They wrote of her: "She lied to kill, but she killed to love."

The pretty twenty-year-old, blonde and poised with blue eyes, was the only daughter of Ernst Beier and Ida Karoline, a well-off Lutheran family. After concluding her studies, she found work in the town hospital.

Her ambitious father arranged her marriage to engineer Karl Pressler, the rich and respected head of the Chemnitz steel-works, in Lower Saxony. Pressler had fallen in love with her when he saw her at a dance and had asked for her hand, even if he might have to wait.

In fact, Karl was twenty years older than she was: his hair was beginning to recede, and he was running to fat. Greta felt disgust rather than love for the man. And her heart beat for

Grete Beier posing with the fiancé, the engineer Karl Pressler.

another: Hans Merker, an unemployed good-for-nothing who had, without deserving it, gained her devotion. But he certainly did not have Herr Beier's respect.

The Eve of the Great Day

The wedding was arranged for May 14th, 1907, but no date alone could affect Grete's determination. First she suggested to her lover that he could stay by her side despite the husband, so as to enjoy the economic benefits of the marriage. However, this was not enough for Hans, who threatened to tell everyone about the affair and two illegal abortions.

"I had to do it. I had no choice," Grete would confess later. On the eve of the great day, she had herself invited to dinner at Karl's house and poured potassium cyanide into his cognac. The poison paralyzed him almost instantly. Then the woman staged a suicide. She blindfolded him with a black band, shot him twice in the mouth, and wrote a farewell letter:

> *I declare my fiancée Grete Beier to be the universal heiress of all my possessions and property. I beg my relatives strongly to forego the portions they are legally entitled to. (...) This is my last will and testament, written and signed in my own hand, in the full possession of my faculties. Be happy, always happy, in this world; I have enjoyed it to the full.*

In one stroke, well-aimed and calculated, Grete had solved the problems of the marriage forced on her and of Merker's continual demands for money. Her heart was suddenly lighter.

> *I was astonished by my calm. I was happy that everything was already done.*

One Theft and One Letter Too Many

Grete ended up almost believing in her sham, and no one questioned anything. She pretended to be shocked by the news and suggested cremating the body, as Karl would have wished. In two days all the potential evidence of her crime seemed to have gone up in smoke.

And yet on June 27th she was served with an arrest warrant. Not for murder, but for theft. Hans continued to demand money, a lot of money, and she had taken some from the treasury of the hospital where she worked. Then a female colleague had put the police on her track. The investigations came thick and fast: Grete would never ever have made trouble for her lover by explaining the reasons for her behavior, but for the investigators it was not difficult to track down the man and to search his house.

Thus it was that in the same way that a false letter had protected Grete from suspicion, another letter, this time authentic, led to her being charged for the murder of Karl Pressler. In Hans' stove, there was a sheet of paper with her writing, which was only scorched at the edges. It asked him for a favor: "Can you free me from Schlegel as I freed you from Pressler?" She wanted to take her revenge on the colleague who had betrayed her, and suggested that her man drug and kill her. The letter had been delivered by her mother, who had gone to visit her in prison, and it had been thrown on the embers, but had not caught fire.

A Confession in Exchange for a Pardon

The young murderess recounted everything during the trial, confessed every detail and admitted her guilt. She had repented

THE KING'S WIFE

The royal family of Saxony, particularly King Georg I, always disapproved of Louise of Hapsburg - Lorraine's daughter-in-law. She paid little attention to court etiquette and formality. She was descended from Maria Teresa of Austria and Charles X of France, and married Crown Prince Friedrich August on November 21st, 1891; but in 1903 a royal decree ordered their divorce. She had in fact abandoned her home and family while she was pregnant with her third child. She lost imperial styles and titles, and on September 25th, 1907, she got married again, to Enrico Toselli, an Italian musician. In contrast, Friedrich August, who ascended the throne in 1904, did not marry again: as a religious man, he did not recognize the validity of divorce.

but could not have acted differently, she said. It was her only way to continue living. She was found guilty: the death penalty, since the murder was premeditated. In Saxony, the death penalty for a woman had not been carried out since 1852.

The jury, which had the possibility of appealing the court's decision, unanimously asked that it be commuted to life imprisonment, but this was rejected. The attorney for the defense requested a pardon from King Friedrich August of Saxony, who could have granted it, since she was a confessed criminal. But the sovereign denied it. The malicious people stated that by this gesture he wanted to avenge himself on all unfaithful women, including his wife.

The psychiatric evidence ordered to assess Grete's sanity read: "Sane, but defective in feeling, in heart." This "half" infirmity was not enough to save her life.

LA DOMENICA DEL CORRIERE

NEL REGNO ESTERO	Si pubblica a Milano ogni Domenica	UFFICI DEL GIORNALE:
Anno . . . . . L. 5 — L. 10.—		Via Solferino, N. 28
Semestre . . . . » 2,75 » 5,25	Supplemento illustrato del "Corriere della Sera „	MILANO

Per tutti gli articoli e illustrazioni è riservata la proprietà artistica e letteraria, secondo le leggi e i trattati internazionali.

| Anno XII — N. 11. | 13 - 20 Marzo 1910. | Centesimi 10 il numero. |

Le cause celebri: l'inizio del processo dei russi alla Corte d'Assise di Venezia per assassinio.

(Disegno di A. Beltrame).

TARNOWSKA
1910

The Trial of the Russians

Maria Tarnovska (Italy)

A treacherous social climber or victim of the obsessions of her many men? The life of Maria Tarnovska, a fascinating Russian aristocrat, was at the center of a complicated trial that had all of Venice talking in the early 1900s.

Молчи – Say nothing. Donat's warning continued to echo in her ears, while her gondola, black as the night, slipped slowly along the Grand Canal. That order, imperious and arrogant, mistaken by the Carabinieri for a greeting, had made her smile. Say nothing. If only it was possible. Say nothing, and do not hear anything either. To be rid of the shouts and insults of the people, the chattering of the journalists, the softly whispered comments of men of every rank and age as she passed. To lose herself in the immense silence of the steppe around her native city, Otrada, or in the unmistakable murmuring of the high birch forests.

They had already said much on her account in any case: Circe, high class prostitute, snake-woman, black angel. They had painted her as a *femme fatale*, an irresistible dominatrix, someone who could seduce with a glance, lift her men to breathtaking heights and dash them inexorably to their ruin. Love, money, death. Three words that had marked her destiny and would, she was sure, immortalize her. Eternal. Like the fascination of the city that was the background of the events of September 4th and was now preparing to judge her.

Illustration of La Domenica del Corriere *in March, 1910, showing the beginning of the trial against Maria Tarnovska and her accomplices.*

Parties, Drugs and Heroic Sacrifices

Maria Nikolaievna O'Rourke, born in Otrada in 1877, was a descendent of an Irish noble family. Her father, Nicolaj Maritievič O'Rourke, was an officer in the navy, while her mother, Ekaterina Petrovna, was a Russian aristocrat.

At seventeen, after breaking the heart of her first fiancé, who then became a priest, Maria ran away from home to marry Count Vasilij Tarnovskij. The couple moved to Kiev and from that day on life was a succession of parties, luxury, and fun for the little Countess.

Her husband took her with him to orgies and parties, flirting openly with other women in front of her and surrounding her with lovers. Unrestrained spending on jewels, clothes and travel soon led to the end of the money that Vasilij had received from his father. The first marital disagreements began.

Soon Maria gave birth to her first child, a son called Vasilij "Tioka". The husband, who had hoped for a daughter, persuaded her to leave the child with his parents and seventeen-year-old brother, Pëtr, in order to go to Milan, to take singing lessons.

During their stay in Italy Tarnovski received a telegram that brought new stress for the couple: Pëtr had hanged himself, perhaps because his beautiful sister-in-law, for whom he had lost his head, had rejected him.

The arrival of a second child, Tatiana, did not bring Maria and Vasilij together again. Indeed, in the course of a duel between her husband and another Russian gentleman, Maria met an attractive officer of the Hussars, Alexis Boržewskij, who promptly fell in love with her. While they were practicing at the shooting range, Alexis put his hand over the muzzle of the pistol that Maria was holding and said:

- *Before pulling the trigger, I want you to say to me: "Alexis I love you."*
- *You are crazy, take your hand away from there!*

A little later a gunshot rang out and blood gushed from the officer's hand. Struck by the gesture, Maria surrendered and an intense and passionate affair began between the two.

Outraged by Tarnovskij's continual public humiliation of his wife by his numerous extramarital adventures, Alexis challenged him to a duel, but he refused. The lover, prompted by the woman, then invited the couple to a reconciliation supper.

We left the Grand Hotel and Boržewskij, thanking us for having accepted the invitation, kissed my hand, then kissed my husband again and we invited him to breakfast. He accompanied us to our sled and, while he helped me to mount, we heard a shot: I felt the whistle of the bullet that parted the fur on my hat. Boržewskij fell at my feet, wounded in the head, staining my cape, dress and shoes with his blood.

The jealous Tarnovskij had shot him. Maria vainly accompanied Alexis to the best European clinics. In Yalta, in the Crimea, Vladimir Stahl, a morphine-addicted doctor who was in love with Maria, injected both her and the lover with morphine. The narcotics sped up the end for Boržewskij and pushed the woman, distraught, into his arms.

After the officer's funeral, however, Maria rejected Stahl. In despair after waiting in vain for her, the doctor killed himself.

The Lawyer, the Millionaire and the Knight

In the meantime, Tarnovskij was arrested for the murder of Boržewskij, and Maria retained a famous Moscow lawyer, Donat Prilukov, to start divorce proceedings. Before meeting Maria, Donat had led a respectable life: he was married with three children, appreciated by clients for his professional ability and generosity. The eruption of Tarnovska into his life, however, changed all that. He wrote:

> *I will follow you wherever you go, I will be where you are. Only death will separate us, because the devils will separate me from your side in fear that you exchange hell for paradise.*

Donat began to spend all his savings on Maria, even going so far as to buy her an apartment in Moscow. Later on he decided to escape abroad with her. Before leaving, he embezzled 80.000 rubles from his clients and officially became an outlaw. Traveling with the couple was little Tioka and Elise Perrier (a Swiss governess employed to look after the child) who was a faithful servant dedicated to her mistress.

Maria went to Dresden for the funeral of a friend of hers, Emilia Roeder. While there she met her widower, the millionaire Count Pavel Kamarovskij who, seduced by her allure, began to put her on a pedestal.

She told Donat of the encounter and he urged her to become more involved with the Count in order to get her hands on his fortune; so it was that when Kamarovskij declared his love for Maria at Orel and asked her to become his fiancé, she accepted.

On that occasion it was the same Kamarovskij who introduced her to her future lover, Nicolaj Naumov. Naumov was twenty-three and a secretary to the governor of Orel: cultured and refined, he was related to Turgenev and already had a Russian translation of Baudelaire to his credit. A fragile and sensitive soul, he was hot-tempered, masochistic, and quickly becoming an alcoholic. He was instantly struck by Maria at their

DEATH IN VENICE BY VISCONTI

Many artists and intellectuals followed the vicissitudes of the Russian Countess and her lovers with interest. In 1943 the directors Luchino Visconti and Antonio Pietrangeli registered the copyright of the subject for a film entitled *Morte a Venezia - Il processo di Maria Tarnowsky* (Death in Venice - the trial of Maria Tarnowsky) with the Italian Copyright Agency (forerunner of the SIAE). Michelangelo Antonioni also participated with Visconti and Pietrangeli in the production of the screenplay. The film was expected to star Isa Miranda and Vittorio Gassman in the main roles, with Venice and Verona as locations and Lux Film as the production company. Visconti studied the case carefully, completing inspections in Venice and documenting the film through books, legal transcripts, and contemporary reports. The breakdown of the relationship with Isa Miranda, wife of the producer of the film on behalf of Lux, led to the cancellation of the project in 1946. The project was revived and reprocessed later, first by Fellini and Pinelli, then by Moravia and Pietrangeli. In the 1960s Visconti returned to the Tarnovska project, planning to involve Romy Schneider and Helmut Berger, but on that occasion, too, the intense activity came to nothing. Visconti's fascination with the "rich greedy international adventurer, drug addict, criminal, with almost hypnotic seductive power, cruel intelligence, pseudo-intellectual artistic interest, petty crime, sadism" is recorded in a book (containing the original screenplay, some photos with Romy Schneider, and the preliminary location search) which is kept with the Luchino Visconti papers archived by the Gramsci Institute Foundation. It is a record of an intense, meticulous reconstruction of an aristocratic, decadent world that has almost completely disappeared.

first meeting: he had her whip him, stub out cigarettes on his skin and even had her initials tattooed on his arm.

Maria's three men found themselves re-united in Venice: Tarnovska, in fact, stayed at the Grand Hotel des Bains, where the Kamarovskij engagement party was held; in an adjoining room, unknown to the Count, was Donat. Not far away, Naumov waited anxiously at the Danieli Hotel to see his beautiful Countess again.

The Russian Crime

Meanwhile, Maria and Donat conspired to get control of the rich fiance's money: Tarnovska convinced Kamarovskij to underwrite a life insurance policy to the value of 500.000 rubles. Then she delivered Naumov a telegram:

> *I know everything. Your Naumov is a no-good. I regret my good feelings towards you because you are a worthless woman.*

Kamarovskij's signature appeared below these words, but they had been written by Donat to provoke the anger of the young man. Naumov fell into the trap and swore to Maria to avenge her.

On September 4th 1907 a man wearing a gray coat knocked on the door of the Palazzo Maurogonato, in Campo Santa Maria del Giglio, asking to be received by Pavel Kamarovskij. The servant answered that the master was sleeping, but the Count recognized the voice of his friend, Naumov. He came to meet him in a dressing gown, with open arms.

Naumov shot him.

Confused, the Count exclaimed:

- What have I done to you?
- Now you will not be able to marry Maria Tarnovska!
- You unfortunate wretch, but don't you know that I have a son who lost his mother a short time ago and now is to lose his father, too?

Struck by Kamarovskij's words, Naumov turned the gun on himself, but could not shoot himself because he had run out of ammunition. He burst into tears and embraced his old friend, only to be told to escape and go somewhere safe. Thanks to the report of the gondolier who had brought him, Naumov was traced by the police and arrested in Verona.

Kamarovskij, seriously wounded, was taken to the hospital. Initially, his condition seemed to improve, but he died four days after the attempted homicide, after a stomach pumping. During his stay in the hospital the Count sent various telegrams to his fiancé asking her to join him and it was through these that the police succeeded in finding the Countess and her lover, who had fled to Vienna.

Trial in Venice

The trial of Maria Tarnovska, otherwise known as the "Case of the Russians", drew world-wide attention due to the strong personality of its main actors. Correspondents from *The New York Times, Novosti, Frankfurter Zeitung, Le Figaro, Il Corriere della Sera*, Edgar Dégas, Gabrielle Réjan, Sarah Bernardt and many others were among the first audience to show up for the trial at the Rialto Court on March 4th 1910. In the dock were seated Maria Tarnovska, Donat Prilukov, Nicolaj Naumov and Elise Perrier.

Tall, elegant, composed, wearing a black dress with Lavallière collar, her face covered by a black veil which fell over her eyes from the wide brim of her hat, Maria maintained an imperturbable calm for the whole length of the trial. It was said that the police escort had to be changed everyday because they were bewitched by her charm. She was insulted and despised by the people: "Tarnovska to the gallows" graffiti appeared on the wall of the Palazzo Maurogonato.

The trial dragged on for two months, and after medical and psychiatric statements, testimony, and technical evidence were given, the verdict was reached at last. Naumov, accused of premeditated murder, was sentenced to prison for 3 years and one month due to extenuating factors (errors by the doctors, mental infirmity, in addition to generic extenuating circumstances). Tarnovska was accused of premeditated murder but, because of the same extenuations, was sentenced to 8 years and 4 months. Prilukov, accused of being an accomplice in the murder in order to commit a further crime, was sentenced to 10 years in prison. Perrier, who initially was accused of complicity, was given a full acquittal.

Flora's Jewels

Andrés Gómez Mena (Cuba)

The man, visibly upset, entered the elegant Manzana de Gómez bar in the center of Havana with all the fury of a tropical cyclone. He headed straight for the armchair where José Gómez Mena, the rich owner of the whole block, was drinking his six-o'clock mojito. "You have two minutes to say your prayers," he screamed, "then I kill you." And he was as good as his word.

Andrés Gómez Mena was a descendent of a Spanish family that had made its fortune in Cuba in the slavery era. Almost a prince in Havana, his cachet wasn't of nobility but, much more prosaic, of money. His "royal palace", the Manzana de Gómez, occupied an entire block in the heart of the capital, and was in fact what would today be called a shopping mall. It was all *Belle-Epoque* elegance with two arcades crossing at right angles, stores, restaurants, even a theater. It was the happy hunting ground for the amorous adventures of young store clerks and beautiful customers. But in one of those stores worked the man who would become a killer: Fernando Reugart, an insignificant watchmaker. He was married to a beautiful woman, Flora.

The Six-o'clock Mojito

Every afternoon, towards six, Gómez Mena could be found at the Manzana bar – his bar, in every sense. He sipped his mojito as an aperitif, accompanied by the flattery and servile gestures of the bartender who rented the premises and was accumulating a small fortune day by day. It was enough that Gómez Mena showed himself at a bar, a restaurant, or a nightclub for that enterprise to be a success.

He was there one afternoon, savoring his mojito, when the door opened and into the bar swept Flora, like a dream. Her hair was made up in an elaborate quasi-Baroque style, her bosom prominent, her look determined. She left almost immediately. A word with the bartender was enough to reveal that she was the wife of the watchmaker – a man whose face Gómez Mena could not remember but who paid his rent regularly.

It may have only been a fleeting moment, but the rich Cuban could not get the vision out of his mind. In the following days, on his way to the bar he invariably passed by the watchmaker's store: sometimes he entered to say hello, feigning interest in goods or customers; other times he paused in front of the window, pretending to be interested in the goods on display, but letting his eye stray to behind the counter. There he saw the bewitching Flora.

A picture from 1940 showing the five-storey building Manzana de Gómez in the Havana Vieja.

Like Cinderella

The watchmaker had just left on a business trip and Gómez Mena had no intention of waiting any longer. He invited Flora to supper and she accepted; she did not object even when he took her in his carriage to his *pied-a-terre*, a little villa out on the coast.

There's an old Havana saying: "Cubans think the worst of people. If we see a woman getting into a car with a fellow, we think they're off to bed. Trouble is, we're usually right!" In the case of Flora it was only too true. A rich, powerful man, fascinating in his own way, had plucked her from the daily grind of the back shop and was treating her like a goddess, like he'd fallen head over heels in love with her, just like in the fairy-tales.

Flora was right. Gómez Mena had fallen in love and in order to show it he began to give her gifts of unbelievably expensive earrings, rings, necklaces. Above all, he gave her jewels to decorate her elaborate hairdo. Flora wore them only for him, when they were together, when in the secrecy of the villa she was transformed into a princess. For the rest, she had no alternative: how would she explain the unexpected blossoming of gold and gems to her husband, to her friends? But her double life began to weigh upon her. She dreamed of one day being able to walk along the streets of colonial Havana on the arm of her man, wearing all the precious stones with which he had declared his eternal love for her, and watching all the passersby die of envy.

Betrayal, Betrayal

Flora hid the jewels in a drawer that only she used. But then, on January 11th, 1917, Fernando, looking for something he had lost, opened the drawer and came upon the hoard of jewels. He immediately knew their value, and his world fell apart. He confronted his wife.

What's the meaning of these jewels? Who gave them to you?

She tried to brazen it out and think of some excuse, but she realized that it was useless. Instead, she thought that this man, who was threatening her and had already struck her, might be reasoned with. Perhaps, if her husband knew who her lover was and what gifts he was prepared to give, he might go along with the betrayal. He might even benefit from a complicity with Gómez Mena.

"Andrés Gómez Mena, the owner of the Manzana, is one of the richest men in Cuba." He stopped for a moment, and looked at his watch. It was almost six o'clock. Shortly it would be time for the customary mojito. He decided to take revenge. He kept a gun to protect himself from thieves. He took it and set off for an appointment with a man who wasn't expecting him. On the stroke of six, Gómez Mena entered the bar, settled into his usual armchair, and was waiting for people to pay their customary respects when, instead, Flora's husband stormed in, mad with jealousy. The man had little to say:

You have two minutes to say your prayers! Then I kill you!

Her Jewels, at Last

The police arrested the killer, and Flora, too, because adultery was a crime. She chose a very popular lawyer, Portocarrero, as her defense council. He was the father of René, who was destined to become one of the best known Latin American painters.

The case created a lot of interest, the newspapers filled page after page with reports on this early soap-opera.

In the end Flora knew that she was going to be released. She called Portocarrero and asked him to bring her all her jewels. She spent the last morning in jail doing up her hair and putting on Gómez Mena's clandestine gifts. When she left the prison by the front gate, where hundreds of people were waiting to catch a glimpse of her, Flora was resplendent. At last she could feel like a princess in the light of day.

FEMINIST ICON

"My father, who was Flora's lawyer, took me to see her when that beautiful lady came out of jail. I was little, but like all those who had waited hours to see her, I was dazzled by such an attractive woman and the multicolored light reflected by her jewelry, ever changing and multiplying the beams of the tropical midday sun." This was how René Portocarrero (1912-85), master of Cuban painting, remembered that unforgettable scene. For years after that, he painted Flora with her elaborate Baroque hairstyle spattered with precious stones. She was to become an icon of the feminist movement in the 1970s.

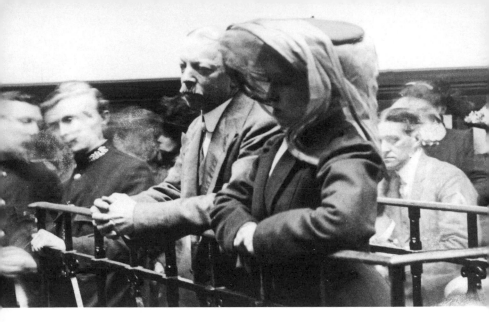

The House of Horrors

Hawley Harvey Crippen (United Kingdom)

In 2007 an American team of researchers discovered that the remains found in Dr. Crippen's cellar did not belong, as people believed, to his wife Cora. But the discovery came too late. The Doctor was hanged in London in 1910, overwhelmed by "undeniable" evidence in the first trial in history dominated by forensic science. His attempt to flee was also stopped by technological progress: for the first time, with this case, a telegraph was used to capture a criminal. But almost a hundred years after Crippen's execution, some think that the investigation, using more advanced techniques, should be carried out again.

Reports of the time describe him as a short man, kind and polite. Hawley Harvey Crippen was born in 1862 in Coldwater, Michigan, into a family of workers who lived by Puritan values. His parents owned a notions shop, thanks to which they were comfortably off. Right from childhood, Hawley showed an interest in medicine. In 1884 he received a degree in homeopathy from Cleveland Homeopathic Medical College. Then he moved to New York, where he met his first wife: a nurse of Irish origin, Charlotte Bell, who was an overzealous Catholic. They had a son, Otto, but in 1892 Charlotte died unexpectedly of an apoplectic fit. The young doctor, now a widower, entrusted the child to the grandparents, who lived in California, and decided to stay in New York to continue his work.

Cora, His Second Wife

In July, 1892, a buxom nineteen-year-old entered Dr. Crippen's office in Brooklyn complaining of "female disorders", the result of an abortion which made her sterile. She came from a family of Polish and German immigrants and her ambition was to break into show business. She called herself Cora Turner, having changed her real family name, Mackamotski, with one more American. The little, bespectacled doctor fell hopelessly in love with the impressive girl, and after two months the two of them were married.

Cora continued to take opera singing lessons without obtaining the results she hoped for. Very soon, her husband's salary proved insufficient for her demands of clothing and jewels, for her thirst for the good life. In 1894 Crippen began working for Munyon's, a homeopathic products company, and shorty afterward they moved to London.

Their London Decline

Dr. Crippen's professional ability opened doors for him in Munyon's London offices, where he soon became a manager.

Hawley Harvey Crippen and the lover Ethel Le Neve behind the dock.

Meanwhile, his wife, with the stage name Belle Elmore, pursued her theater career, but found very little success. Her husband supported her by giving her large sums of money, and by working on his own career. Although they lived well in the elegant district of Bloomsbury, Cora's chronic dissatisfaction and her uncontrolled spending undermined the stability of the couple.

When homeopathy became unfashionable and there was no more work at Munyon's, Dr. Crippen found himself in serious trouble. Economic problems forced them to move to 19 Hilldrop Crescent, in Camden Town, a very large house which they partly rented. Cora continued to perform in the city's cabarets and to hang around with bad company: while her career did not take off, she had become a kind of celebrity because of her irrepressible vitality, her bizarre hairstyles and showy dresses. Rumor had it that she openly collected lovers. Her marriage to Crippen was, soon enough, on the rocks. To console himself, the shy Dr. Crippen began a relationship, initially platonic, with Ethel Le Neve, a young secretary. With her he found a little calm. The situation dragged along for some years: Crippen didn't decide to break up with Cora, who nevertheless wanted to avoid the scandal of a divorce.

Cora's Disappearance

Cora was last seen on January 31st, 1910. There had been a little party at the Crippens', attended by a retired actor and his wife and a couple of Cora's friends. It was the acquaintances who first became suspicious about Cora's disappearance, which her husband explained by claiming she had returned to the United States where, soon after arriving, she had died of pneumonia and been cremated. But, stranger still, Ethel Le Neve had begun to live in the house, rapidly replacing the deceased woman, and wearing her dresses and jewels. The idyll lasted for six months. Then, under pressure from the circle of friends, unable to come to terms with the fact that she left without giving any notice and didn't bring her riches along, the police intervened. Dr. Crippen was interrogated by inspector Walter Dew (well known for having investigated the unresolved case of Jack the Ripper twenty years before). Crippen confessed to lying about Cora: she had, in fact, gone off with a lover. The house was searched, but nothing was found.

In a panic, the doctor and his new companion fled to Brussels, and then Antwerp, where they embarked on a ship, the *Montrose*, bound for Canada. Ethel disguised herself as a man to avoid being recognized. They did not know that the police had been satisfied after that first visit. It was precisely their rapid flight which revived suspicions about their possible involvement in Cora's disappearance.

The Truth Comes to Light

Inspector Dew had returned to Hilldrop Crescent to ask Crippen some more questions. When he realized they had fled, he launched a manhunt and searched the building more carefully. He hit the bull's eye. In the basement, under the brick floor, human remains were discovered: chest and abdomen organs. It was impossible to determine the sex. Only a fragment of skin, with what seemed to be a scar, would prove decisive in the identification of Cora's body. The head, the legs, and the skeleton were never found.

After the alert of Scotland Yard, the captain of the *Montrose*, Henry George Kendall, realized the two fugitives were on his ship: it was Ethel's bad disguise that attracted his attention, and he promptly gave the alarm, which began the use of the telegraph as a means in the capture of criminals.

While the news appeared on the front page of the newspapers, arousing international attention, the passengers of the ship were kept in the dark about what was happening.

Inspector Dew rushed off in pursuit, on a ship that reached Quebec before the *Montrose*. "Good day, Dr. Crippen, do you recognize me? I'm inspector Dew of Scotland Yard". And Crippen replied:

> *Thank God it's over. The suspense was too great. I couldn't stand it any longer.*

The doctor gave himself up without a fight. It was July 31st, 1910. Crippen's trial for murder began on October 18th, while Ethel Le Neve was tried separately. During five days in court, pathologists succeeded in demonstrating that the mass of organs belonged to Cora (there was a scar, hair, and the remains of some pajamas). Other evidence considered conclusive was the purchase shortly before the wife's disappearance of a considerable quantity of hyoscine, a toxic substance of which traces were found on the torso. According to the prosecution, the doctor killed his wife with this.

The defense reiterated the theory of Cora's leaving with another man, and suggested that a previous lodger could have been responsible for the crime and buried the body of an unknown person. It contested the scientific evidence, and also maintained that the mark on the tissue sample (on the basis of which the identification of the body had been made) could not be a scar because hair was growing over it. It was all to no avail. The jury only took 27 minutes to pronounce a guilty verdict.

On November 25th, 1910, Dr. Crippen was hanged in Pentonville Prison in London. Ethel was acquitted, and on the day of the execution left for the United States under an assumed name.

The house of horrors, as it was depicted in newspapers of the time, was razed to the ground during the Second World War by German bombing.

The Surprise of DNA

In 2007 John Trestrail, an American forensic toxicologist who was not convinced of Crippen's guilt, decided to investigate the case again. What could not be explained was why Crippen would have left part of Cora's body instead of getting rid of it completely. Additionally, those who administer a poison usually try to pass the murder off as a natural death or an accident.

THE SECRETS TO THE GRAVE

After fleeing to New York, and living for awhile in Toronto, Ethel Le Neve returned to London in 1915, where she married and had two children. She died there in 1967, at the age of eighty-four. It is said that the most famous lover of the century asked to be buried with a portrait of Dr. Crippen on her heart. When she died, she certainly took many secrets with her. The crime historian Jonathan Goodman noted this when he contacted Ethel's children in the 1980s to write a book on the case. He asked them for an interview, "to put an end to the many legends associated with the death of Crippen." But Bob and Nina, Goodman recounts, "didn't know what I was talking about."

Some fragments of the body, preserved in the London archives, were recovered and a great granddaughter of Cora's was found for comparison. Trestrail requested analysis of DNA, which was then conducted by David Foran in a lab at Michigan State University.

According to the results, the corpse was not Cora's. Furthermore, the claim that the doctor practiced illegal abortions and that the torso belonged to a deceased patient was refuted by the fact that the remains, according to the results, did not even belong to a woman. In the light of the new evidence emerging, James Patrick Crippen, a descendant of Dr. Crippen, requested that the British Government absolve Dr. Crippen posthumously and deliver his ancestor's remains to his family in the USA. The requests were denied by the Criminal Cases Review Commission after a review of the case in 2009. For the law, Dr. Crippen remains guilty.

In the Shade of the Crabapple Tree

Edward Wheeler Hall and Eleanor Mills
(United States)

One mild September morning in 1922, a young man and woman went for a romantic walk along De Russey's Lane in the New Jersey countryside. They never imagined that they would be caught up in an historic American mystery, the eccentric characters of which would become famous far beyond the borders of the United States.

The lifeless bodies of the plump, forty-one-year-old Reverend Edward Wheeler Hall, of the church of Saint John the Evangelist in New Brunswick, and his lover, the slight thirty-four-year-old choir singer Eleanor Mills, were found lying supine in a field under a crabapple tree. The bodies had been arranged with care: their feet were towards the tree and they had been positioned *post mortem* in such a way as to suggest a certain intimacy between them. A panama hat covered the man's face and there was a scarf wrapped around the woman's neck. A single .32 caliber bullet had put an end to the Reverend's life, while the choir singer was killed by three shots to the head and her throat had been cut from ear to ear. Years later, a second autopsy revealed that besides having her throat cut, the killer had also severed her tongue.

To complete the macabre picture, love letters that the two had exchanged were found torn and scattered all around. Publicized extracts of these scandalized Puritan America:

> . . . *I want to look into your dear face for hours while you hold my body close* wrote

the "gypsy queen" to her "babykins", as they called each other in their letters.

Double Jurisdiction

The investigation was confused from the start. The crime scene was on the border between the counties of Middlesex and Somerset. The police from New Brunswick (Middlesex) arrived first, but where the bodies were found was in fact in Franklin District (Somerset).

While the jurisdiction problem was being resolved, curious passersby walked all over the scene, took souvenirs, and seriously contaminated the evidence: the business card found at the feet of Reverend Hall, that had enabled his identification, passed from hand to hand dozens of times.

Nobody did anything to preserve the crime scene, even when the apple tree was pulled down and torn to pieces. Later, the

On the left, Edward Wheeler Hall; on the right, a picture of the place where the corpses of the Reverend and of his lover, Eleanor Mills, had been found.

police didn't have much to base their investigation on. Even though other hypotheses were considered, jealousy of one of the two spouses seemed to be the most reasonable motive. The relationship between the victims had been common knowledge to the entire community for a long time. Eleanor Mills' husband, James, not as naïve as he would have people believe, benefited from his wife's clandestine relationship: Hall had made him sacristan. He was quickly ruled out as a suspect because he had spent the evening of the murder in a bar.

Suspicion then fell on the Reverend's wife, Mrs. Frances Stevens Hall. She was seven years older than her husband, and while she certainly could not compete with Eleanor Mills for looks, she made up for what she lacked in charm by being well connected: her family was one of wealthiest in New Brunswick. It was no secret that the parish priest had married her for her money. Her brothers were also investigated: William "Willie" Carpender Stevens (who owned a .32 caliber like the one used in the murder) and Henry Hewgill Stevens, a retired sharpshooter. They had motive, means and opportunity. Even an eyewitness, Jane Gibson, had come forward.

But as a result of the first superficial investigation led by Joseph E. Stricker – in the course of which many mouths were closed by the influential Stevens family – no formal indictments were brought and the case was closed.

If it had not been for an angry husband and an ambitious news-editor, the matter would probably have been forgotten. But four years later, as a result of a media campaign, the investigation was reopened and the case was back in the limelight.

The Pig Woman

In seeking the annulment of his marriage to Louise Geist, who had been a servant in the Hall household, Mr. Arthur Riehl claimed to have learned from her that Rev. Hall had tried to

---

BETWEEN TRUTH AND FICTION

The Hall-Mills case is particularly famous in the history of journalism for the international level of media coverage: the international press dedicated more space to it than to any other American penal procedure. The record would stand until the Lindbergh Kidnapping trial (also held in New Jersey) in the 1930s. Already by 1925 the silent film *The Goose Woman* used the Jane Gibson story. But much has been written since on "the crabapple case", from journalist Damon Runyon to the crime writer Mary Roberts Rinehart. The trial inspired the novels *The Crime*, by Stephen Longstreet, and *The Bellamy Trial*, by Frances Noyes Hart, a pioneering work of the legal thriller genre which was brought to the big screen in 1929.

More than forty years after the murder, the celebrated activist and lawyer William Kunstler entered the debate with a new theory, the subject of his 1964 book *The Minister and the Choir Singer* (updated and reissued in 1980 as *The Hall-Mills Murders*). Kunstler suggests that the adulterous couple had violated the moral code of the Ku Klux Klan, who would have killed them for that. But it is only one of dozens of theories, including some that have the Pig Woman as the true killer.

In the 1999 Gerald Tomlinson published *Fatal Tryst*, the most detailed investigation written on the case until now, while a detailed report of the impact of the murder on the community can be found in the works of William B. Brahms. Finally, in her 2013 book *Careless People*, Sarah Churchwell speculates that part of the finale of Fitzgerald's *The Great Gatsby* (1925) was based on the Hall-Mills case. Even today books are still being published on the case. And some still believe that the killer can be identified.

escape with his lover and that he had been followed by his wife, her brothers and a cousin, Henry de la Bruyere Carpender. According to Riehl, Geist had received $ 5000 to keep quiet.

The man's claim reached the city newspaper, W. R. Hearst's *New York Daily Mirror*. Philip Payne, the managing editor, saw the occasion as a means of increasing sales, and he used every strategy of yellow journalism to have the investigation reopened. The headlines screamed: "The truth of the mystery revealed by the Mirror!" and a new trial date was quickly set. Frances Hall, Willie, and Henry Stevens were taken to court in November, 1926.

Everything depended on the evidence of Jane Gibson, a middle-aged country woman who lived near the crime scene. She raised pigs and came to be referred to as Pig Woman. Four years before, nobody had listened to her.

Although Gibson was in the hospital being treated for cancer, the procurator Alexander Simpson insisted that she testify: she was brought into the courtroom on a gurney, from which she gave her version of the events. She became the star of the trial.

Two evenings before the discovery of the bodies, she heard unusual noises and left her house on her mule Jenny to check on what she thought might be a maize thief. Instead, getting closer, she saw a group of people and overheard a bitter argument between two men and two women. She hid, and heard someone say,

You explain these letters to me!

Shots were followed by a scream, and first one and then another figure fell to the ground, dead. Gibson then withdrew, terrified, but not before she heard a woman scream the name Henry.

The Verdict

The defense claimed there were a number of discrepancies in the account given by the Pig Woman from one deposition and to another, and so she could not be considered reliable. They painted the witness as a boorish idiot to demolish her credibility. And the fact that her own mother, sitting in the front row, continually repeated "Liar" did not help Gibson.

The prosecution hoped that at least Willie, once put to the test, would break down. The widow Hall's eccentric brother had a walrus mustache, and instead of working he hung out with a group of local fireman, wearing his own home-made uniform. But Willie answered all the questions, was sure and convincing, and showed the same controlled composure as his sister.

Thus, after five hours of deliberation, the evidence was found to be insufficient. The jury acquitted Mrs. Hall and her brothers. The accusation against the cousin, who would have had to be tried separately, was withdrawn. The trial concluded, but "the crabapple case" remained unsolved, and the mystery of who killed the Pastor and the choir singer survives to the present day.

The Lover in the Attic

Walburga Oesterreich (United States)

When the incredible story of Walburga Oesterreich and her young lover-slave Otto Sanhuber became public, the newspapers dubbed Otto "the batman", as for seven years he had lived in an attic. And for years, Oesterreich's husband, Fred, had unknowingly harbored under his roof, literally, the man who satisfied his wife's insatiable sexual appetite. For him, it would have been better if he had never discovered it.

In 1913 Walburga, known as Dolly, was a woman of about thirty-five who had been married for more than ten years to Fred Oesterreich, the rich owner of a textile company in Milwaukee.

The Oesterreichs, both of German origin, had different temperaments: Fred, a few years older, was an arrogant and obsessive man dedicated to his work and given to drinking. Dolly was vivacious and sensual, so full of desire that multiple lovers weren't enough to satisfy her.

While visiting her husband's factory one day, Dolly noticed the seventeen-year-old Otto Sanhuber, a slight boy who was repairing a sewing machine. Maybe she was encouraged by the passionate prospects of his youth, maybe by his awkward immaturity. At the first opportunity, she invited him to her home with an excuse. Otto was shy and sexually inexperienced. He was received by a mature, provocative woman wearing only a dressing gown. And that was enough.

Their affair was explosive, torrid, and perverse, and kept the lovers busy for many hours of the day while Fred was at work. But it did not pass unobserved by the neighbors, who soon sowed suspicion in the mind of the oblivious husband.

The Batman

Walburga devised a faultless solution: she persuaded her young lover, who was an orphan, to give up his job. Then she moved him into her attic, so as to have him always available. Obviously, she did this without Fred knowing.

Incredibly, the new arrangement continued for a few years with no major problems, although Otto was subject to attacks of jealousy, especially when he helplessly witnessed the couple's intimacy directly beneath his hiding place. For his part, several times Fred was on the point of venturing into that forgotten attic to investigate the nature of the strange noises and coughs that disturbed him in the middle of the night. But Dolly, imperturbable and clever, deflected Fred's suspicions, attributing the "hallucinations" and the strange disappearance of food to

Walburga Osterreich's first arrest in 1923; on her right, the detective Herman Cline.

his drinking. Finally, she persuaded him to move in order to regain his peace of mind, and arranged everything so that Otto could follow them unobserved to another . . . attic.

Meanwhile, the boy, despite his small size, ate in proportion to the frequency of his sexual performances. During the day, when he was not busy satisfying Walburga, he helped her with the housework; at night, shut in his little room, he wrote adventure and fantasy stories by an oil lantern, and published under a pseudonym.

Murderer and Handyman

In 1918, when the Oesterreichs decided to move yet again, Dolly made great efforts to find a suitable house in Los Angeles. Otto said this about life in that period:

> They loved to sleep in clean sheets, and I made the bed, tidied their clothes, brushed Fred's suits [...] and polished his shoes, so that he always looked sharp. When [Fred] wasn't at home, I washed the dishes, otherwise he washed them and Mrs. Oesterreich dried them, because I couldn't do it. I washed the vegetables, and they were always clean. Everybody complimented her on the cleanliness of her things.

Their life together was perfect for Otto, who by now thought no other life or loves possible. But something was beginning to crack. In the new home the couple slept in separate rooms, and their marriage was stormy, perhaps because of Dolly's continual deceptions or Fred's constant drinking: there were continuous quarrels.

On August 22nd, 1922, the Oesterreichs came home in the middle of a quarrel. From his hiding place Otto heard their voices rising more and more, and then a more dramatic noise prompted him to intervene, because he feared that his lover was in danger. The boy came down from the attic grasping two .25 caliber pistols, which Dolly had probably given him. Here the story gets confused: perhaps Fred attacked Otto, perhaps Fred didn't have time. What is certain is that several shots rang out, and Fred's heavy body fell lifeless to the floor.

When the chief detective of the Los Angeles Police Department, Herman Cline, reached the scene, he found Dolly in a closet locked from the outside, which precluded her being accused of murder. In fact, how could she have locked herself in the cupboard, with the key lying on the floor? Thus, since they had no reason to suspect the presence of an accomplice, the detective had to accept the version of the events described by the woman: the murder was committed by burglars, who had stolen Fred's diamond-studded watch. But some things could not be explained, above all the bullets that had killed Fred. In fact, no burglar would have used a .25 caliber pistol, a typically female weapon – and that woman, too roguish and showy, was not really convincing to Cline. He carried on with the investigation.

The Widow and Her Attorney

Meanwhile the merry new widow, regardless of Otto's availability in the attic, began an affair with Herman Shapiro, the lawyer who was dealing with her husband's estate. As usual, she cleverly hit upon a way to get rid of the two pistols: she gave one to a neighbor, who promised to get rid of it, and gave the second to an actor friend – perhaps another lover – and explained to him that, in view of recent events, keeping it at home could create problems for her. The friend threw the weapon into the La Brea tar pits, where many of Hollywood's dark secrets have been buried.

Some time afterward, Dolly gave Shapiro the valuable watch which she had reported stolen, probably with the aim of getting rid of it. However, it was this move that gave Cline the means to expose the sham and that enabled him to arrest the woman for homicide. When he learned from the newspapers that Dolly had been arrested, the actor given one of the pistols went to tell the police that she had given him a .25 caliber pistol, and that he had gotten rid of it. But his statement accomplished little. According to some sources, it would be impossible to retrieve the weapon from the pits. According to another account, the pistol was retrieved, but in such a condition that it was useless as evidence.

From prison, Dolly asked Shapiro to go to her house with food and water, and to knock three times on the hidden entrance to the attic behind a cupboard. It was in this way, after a long time, that Otto met someone different from his lover. He opened up, telling a surprising story about the last ten years of his life. Dismayed by this discovery, Shapiro reported everything to Dolly's defense attorney, Frank Dominiquez, who suggested persuading the undesired guest to disappear. Thus Otto, for the good of his lover, left the state and, after ten years in hiding, returned to a normal life. Dolly was released due to lack of evidence.

A Belated Solution

Only in 1930, following a violent break-up with Dolly, did Shapiro decide to confess to Cline what he knew about the incred-

THE ASPIRING WRITER

In the years in which Otto Sanhuber lived cooped up in the Oesterreichs' attics, he was able to give free rein to his ambition to be a writer. He wrote at night in pencil, so as not to make noise, and Walburga then typed up his stories. Otto even became fairly successful by publishing pulp stories in popular magazines. He thus contributed to the "family" income.

ible story of the man who had lived hidden in the Oesterreichs' attics for ten years.

The case was re-opened. Otto, who in the meantime had changed his name and made a life for himself with another woman, was charged, together with his former lover, with first-degree murder. His incredible testimony of his years of sex mixed with housework convinced the jury of his subservience to Dolly. The charge against him was thus reduced to second-degree murder, and since the crime had lapsed, Otto was acquitted.

As for Dolly, the jury was unable to reach a unanimous verdict. Since the murder weapon and concrete evidence against her were lacking, the spry sixty year old avoided conviction once again.

Walburga Oesterreich thus ended her days as a free woman, in fact and in spirit: she died in 1961 at eighty years old, two weeks after marrying her second husband, Ray Bert Hedrick.

Fatal Letters

Edith Graydon Thompson and Frederick Bywaters
(United Kingdom)

Words had always obsessed her. On the pages of books, in countless letters to her "darlingest boy", she had been carried away by them. But at the moment, the words seared her brain. Her mother cried out in despair and rushed for her; her father, defeated and powerless, tried to hold her back. Edith began to scream, to twist and turn and lash out. Then she and Frederick were led down to the cells where they would spend their last weeks of life.

The Thompson house was in disarray. Departure for summer vacation was imminent. Their suitcases were stacked in the corridors, the shutters were closed, and their excitement was evident in their hurried rushing from one room to another. Shanklin, on the Isle of Wight, would be like an oasis for the Thompsons. There, as they did every year, they could escape the routine of everyday life.

Edith Graydon Thompson eagerly awaited the arrival of her sister, Avis, who was to travel with them. Edith was looking forward to spending some time with her and getting some relief from her marriage to Percy, which was slowly wearing her down. That cold, rigid, listless man stifled her vitality, and forced her to retreat into a bourgeois conventional world that she found suffocating. Unknown to Edith, there would be someone else to distract her from her preoccupation. Her sister Avis was bringing along one of her friends, a merchant seaman called Frederick Bywaters.

During the vacation, an extraordinary rapport developed quickly between Edith and Frederick: in long conversations together he told her of his travels, she spoke about her books, her heroines, and her life. They played tennis, swam in the sea, went on excursions; their age difference (she was twenty-eight, he eighteen) was forgotten and their friendship blossomed into something more.

Avis, unaware of the affair between her sister and Frederick, but accepting the young man's lack of interest in herself, gave up. The husband, on the other hand, began to regard the relationship between his better half and the young sailor with growing suspicion. This eventually degenerated into violent arguments between husband and wife. Frederick – alarmed by Edith's cries – tried to intervene. Percy, more furious than ever, drove him from the house.

Edith Graydon Thompson and Frederick Bywaters.

Later, the two lovers tried to persuade Percy to grant Edith a divorce, but Percy flatly refused. The man, who was unhappy about the differences in character and social standing between his wife and himself (she already had an established career and earned far more than her husband), flatly refused: in fact, he feared society gossip and he did not want his reputation to be ruined by a scandal.

Despite everything, Edith was determined to continue her affair with Freddie, because, as she wrote to him:

He has right by law over all that you should have by right of nature and love.

The separation caused by the boy's frequent sea voyages was overcome by a constant correspondence in which the two lovers exchanged literary opinions, emotions, reports of everyday life, and promises. As time went by, however, Edith's letters began to hint at abortion, poisoning, and attempted homicide:

He complained that the tea had a bitter taste "as if someone had put something in it," he said. Now, whatever I use will have a bitter taste. He will recognize it and become still more suspicious. I will try again with glass. This time I will use a light bulb.

However, their situation remained unchanged. So Frederick decided to take things into his own hands.

On the evening of 3rd October, 1922, Edith and her husband went out together to see a show at the Criterion Theater. As they were returning home along a dark deserted street, someone suddenly jumped out, stabbed Percy in the back with a dagger and ran off, leaving him on the ground, dying. Edith ran in desperation to look for help, but when she returned to the scene of the attack, it was too late: Percy was dead.

The woman was taken to a police station, and there, still in shock, she mentioned Frederick Bywaters by name for the first time. The young man was traced and arrested. Because of the letters which were found, both were accused of murder and tried at the Old Bailey in London.

Truth or Fiction?

Public opinion was initially outraged by the behavior of someone labeled an adulteress, abortionist and murderer. But later they were equally riveted by the steadfastness of Frederick, who proclaimed Edith's complete innocence and who assumed all responsibility for the crime.

In the course of the trial, extracts from the correspondence between the two lovers were read. The references to attempted poisoning were the determining factor in convincing the jury

TANGO LESSONS WITH HITCHCOCK

Alfred Hitchcock, one of the many writers and artists who followed the Thompson-Bywaters case closely and whose work was inspired by it, had a direct link with Edith. His family was friendly with the Graydons, parents of Edith and Avis. The father had even given him tango lessons at the Golden Lane Institute. The director's sister kept up her friendship with Avis, and the three met years later. Although they do not appear to have discussed the case, Hitchcock confessed that he would have liked to make a documentary about what happened. In the end, the documentary was never made, but many claim to see various references to the story of the two lovers in the plot of *Stage Fright* (1950).

of the woman's guilt. In fact, an autopsy carried out on Percy Thompson showed no traces of poison or glass. The references were more likely fantasies of Edith's imagination or attempts to sustain Frederick's interest.

Edith was judged on the basis of the principle of common purpose, according to which, if two people conspire in a criminal enterprise, both are equally guilty of the result of that enterprise, regardless of who actually commits the crime. The jury found them both guilty and they were sentenced to death.

Public opinion was mobilized. Approximately a million signatures were collected to ask for the sentence to be commuted, but Home Secretary William Bridgeman, the minister responsible, refused.

On January 9th, 1923, Edith Thompson and Frederick Bywaters were hanged. Their executions were carried out simultaneously in the separate prisons of Holloway and Pentonville. Edith was in a state of semi-consciousness and had to be carried physically to the place of execution; Frederick continued to proclaim her innocence up to the last moment of his life.

The Hollywood Mystery

Thomas H. Ince (United States)

San Diego Pier. Dawn, November 17th, 1924. A stretcher with the dying producer Thomas H. Ince is lowered from millionaire William Randolph Hearst's yacht and loaded into an ambulance. The man dies a few days later, officially from natural causes. But in Hollywood, gossip and rumors begin to circulate, and suspicion grows. What follows is a plausible reconstruction of what actually happened.

Marion Davies' parties were legendary in Hollywood. The actress invented new themes and settings to surprise her guests every time: from bullfighting Spain to the circus, from Oktoberfest to kiddie parties, where everyone dressed up as children. And for every occasion, convoys of movie people would snake down the Pacific Coast from Los Angeles to San Simeon, where the Davies lived. But the Saint Simeon spread, with its fifty-six rooms and nineteen salons, indoor and outdoor swimming pools, tennis courts and even a zoo, was in fact owned by the newspaper magnate William Randolph Hearst.

W. R. had been infatuated with Marion since first seeing her on Broadway in 1917, and to win her over he quickly went about producing a film in which she could star. Marion was twenty-one, had angelic looks and a quick wit; W. R. was fifty-five, controlled an economic empire, and had a wife and five children. The ways of love are mysterious, and here lightning had truly struck. It was said that Hearst was quite possessive of Marion, that his wife Millicent knew of the affair and held her husband in check with exorbitant financial demands, that now

Marion Davies posing beside William Randolph Hearst during one of the legendary theme-parties organized by the woman.

"I AM AN AUTHORITY ON HOW TO MAKE PEOPLE THINK"*

All Hollywood feared William Randolph Hearst. The only one who, many years later, dared to make fun of him was Orson Welles. In 1941 he wrote, directed and starred in *Citizen Kane*, a movie based on the figure of Hearst. Considered a masterpiece in the history of the cinema, the film paints a pitiless portrait of the tycoon. Tyrannical, obsessive, unscrupulous, with a hypertrophic ego, Welles' Kane is driven by violent passions and prepared to manipulate the masses to further his own interests.

* *Citizen Kane* (1941)

and then Marion would cheat on him, and that Patricia, the actress' little niece, was really the secret daughter of the couple. But no badmouthing seemed to upset their happiness. The only thing that counted in Hollywood was spectacle, and Marion's parties were always spectacular.

The Unwelcome Guest

In November, 1924, the caravan of sequins and glitter moved onto Hearst's yacht *Oneida*, for a birthday party for the producer Thomas H. Ince. Hearst wanted to relaunch Cosmopolitan Productions, which he had set up to take Marion to the top of the celluloid Olympus, but which had never taken root in the parched earth of California (nor, in fact, did it ever launch the career of its would be star). He had, therefore, decided to entrust the studio to the direction of Ince, whose string of successful western productions ten years before had played a significant part in the birth of the Hollywood myth. More recently, Ince's reputation had clouded over, but the press baron still had confidence in him. To seal the agreement, Hearst organized an exclusive party-cruise. The guests included close friends of the producer, Marion's two sisters, two journalists who worked for Hearst, a few businessmen, a few starlets – and Charlie Chaplin.

Hearst couldn't stand Chaplin. With his incomprehensible Cockney accent and that smug smile, he showed up punctually at every Saint Simeon party and had begun to orbit Marion. One evening, exasperated by the fact that Marion and Chaplin had been talking earnestly together for more than an hour, W. R. demanded an explanation. Marion shrugged and explained: "Charlie insists on acting with me. He says that I have comic talent and that I should give up melodrama". Hearst lowered his eyes and did not reply, terribly offended in his feelings because he had chosen the scripts for Cosmopolitan.

So, when Marion invited Chaplin to Ince's party, Hearst didn't have the courage to object.

The Dance Begins

Sunday, November 16th, 1924. The sky was clear, the sun was lukewarm and the *Oneida* was sailing steadily south. All the guests were gathered at the stern where Hearst was engaged in one of his favorite games: shooting seagulls with a revolver. That morning he had missed twice. Red with embarrassment, he wiped his hand on his trousers, took a tighter grip on the butt of the gun, squinted along the barrel, and fired. The flight of the bird ended suddenly and it fell into the sea with a dull splash, drowned out by the uproarious applause of the onlookers. Below deck the waiters could be heard uncorking the champagne. Led by Marion, who for the occasion was wearing a jaunty sailor's cap, the company set off prattling towards the ladder that led down to the wide mahogany paneled stateroom where everything was ready for the party. The guests were seated along the table, Hearst presiding over one end, with Marion at the other. The magnate did not miss the catlike movement with which the lean Chaplin had cornered the seat beside Marion.

The lunch passed gaily amidst endless platters of food and rivers of champagne. The company was well matched and the comic exchanges between the old growler W. R. and the impertinent Marion provoked general hilarity.

A jazz quartet began to play and Hearst, his eyes shining with desire and alcohol, headed for his mistress, took her by the hand and led her to the center of the floor to lead the dance. After two circuits of the floor the quartet picked up the rhythm. Old Hearst had to yield to the youngsters and Marion was immediately snapped up by Chaplin. The two tore off into a furious quickstep: they were so much in tune it seemed that they were one person reflected in a mirror. At the end of the dance they were greeted by thunderous applause. Chaplin whispered something into Marion's ear. She burst out laughing and tossed back her blond curls.

Hearst's eyes are glued to the pair and when he sees how Chaplin is looking at Marion's bare neck he feels he's suffocating. The sea seems to rise up suddenly and he nearly loses his balance. Panic pierces his chest from side to side. Why had he let himself be trapped in such a disastrous situation? How could he have been so stupid as to cage himself on a boat with Marion and her lover – with no escape, without the luxury of being able to deceive himself that nothing was happening?

He excused himself to Ince, who was beside him, left the party and went up to the bridge. The sun was lower now and the sea was leaden. He could not bear to lose Marion, nor could he allow Chaplin to take her away from him.

Curiosity Killed the Cat

In Hollywood it was rumored that Thomas H. Ince had had a corridor built over the guest rooms in his Dias Dorados villa on Benedict Canyon Drive, to spy on the his guests' intimacy. Whether this secret corridor ever existed we cannot now know but, as a man of the cinema, Ince was without doubt a keen observer and, no less important, a man with a passionate interest in history. So, that evening, he had not missed a single frame of

THE MOST HATED PEN IN HOLLYWOOD

At the end of the 1800s and the beginning of the 1900s, William Randolph Hearst and Joseph Pulitzer engaged in a no-holds-barred battle for supremacy in the information and newspaper world. The two newspaper tycoons used sensationalism to attract ever greater numbers of readers: this was how the "yellow press" got its start. Articles were based on gossip and unsubstantiated – at times even completely fictitious – claims, and these were always reported with screaming headlines. This conferred enormous power on Hearst, who was essentially in a position to ruin the career of anyone he chose. Such power was not diminished after what happened on the *Oneida*. Indeed, to keep her quiet, Hearst made journalist Louella Parsons the movie critic for the *Los Angeles Examiner*, and Parsons took to the job with unsurpassed zeal. Eventually she would become the journalist most feared by generations of Hollywood stars. She was the weapon that Hearst could point at the head of anyone who disagreed with him.

the Hearst-Davies jealousy drama. He watched Hearst watch Chaplin watch Marion; he had seen his future associate fume with anger while Chaplin watched Marion with the eyes of a predator watching the prey.

And when the two slipped away behind the door that led to the cabins, Chaplin with his arm around Marion's waist, he had no hesitation in following them. "Just protecting the investment", he said to himself to justify.

Marion and Chaplin had disappeared, but a few minutes later Davies reappeared, crossed the floor full of dancers with a determined step, and went up the ladder onto the deck. Ince followed. He had to talk to her, to warn her about committing an indiscretion, because W. R. would never forgive her.

An unexpectedly icy wind struck his face. A November fog

enveloped the *Oneida* and it took Ince a few seconds to make out the slim silhouette of Marion standing at the bow by the rail. He approached her with an uncertain step, leaning into the wall of the bridge against the roll of the boat. Then a shot rang out in the darkness. Ince fell to the deck, mortally wounded.

An Event that Remains a Mystery

Realizing his mistake, Hearst tried desperately to get Ince to a hospital in Saint Diego. But two days later, the man died. According to the official hospital report it was a case of acute indigestion which led to cardiac arrest. The body was cremated immediately, making an autopsy impossible.

Hearst did not attend Ince's funeral but did open a generous fund to support Nell Ince, who, following the funeral, left for a long tour of Europe.

Nothing was ever revealed about that tragic night on the *Oneida* because nobody present ever released any statement. Those present included Louella Parsons, who, though she would soon become one the most feared and pitiless gossip reporters in Hollywood, never wrote a single word about that mysterious cruise and even denied ever having set foot on the yacht.

Marion Davies would never make a film with Charlie Chaplin. Some years later, however, she would turn her back on melodrama in favor of comedy, and become one of the most irresistible comic actresses in the history of Hollywood. She and Hearst would remain together for the rest of their lives. When misfortune befell Hearst at the end of the 1930s, Marion would not hesitate to sell her jewelry to help him out. And a few years later she would withdraw completely from the public eye to be with Hearst, who was by then a sick man.

The Blond Devil

Ruth Brown Snyder (United States)

When Ruth Brown married Albert Snyder, she thought she was a lucky woman. She did not imagine how boring and frustrating her life would soon become. And so, right from the moment she met Judd Gray, a dangerous idea began to whirl in her head.

In 1914 Ruth Brown – tall, blond, radiant – was a nineteen-year-old determined to make something of herself. She worked as a switchboard operator while she studied typing and shorthand. One day she connected the wrong person, apologized to the irate customer, and thus got to know Albert Snyder, the art director of the nautical magazine *Motor Boating*. Thirteen years older than Ruth, Snyder first hired her in his office, and then married her.

In a short time, Ruth had everything that every woman dreamed of: a husband with an excellent salary, a daughter – little Lorraine, born in 1918 – and a three-story house in Queens Village on Long Island.

But she was isolated in the suburbs. When the dinners and parties had finished, she began to feel terribly bored and to hate her life as a housewife. Albert turned out to be a man of few words, introverted but capable of violent outbursts. He spent most of his time away from home because of work, and when he came back he almost ignored his wife. He was even cold to Lorraine. And, more than anything, he could not forget his old fiancée, Jessie Guishard, who had been dead for ten years when he married Ruth. He missed her so much that he named his

Ruth Brown Snyder behind bars in Queens Count Jail.

boat after her, and kept a photo of her hanging in the bedroom, despite Ruth's resentment.

She was the best woman I've ever known. It's a pity you can't be like her

he told his wife again and again.

A Fatal Meeting

To escape her unsatisfying marriage, Ruth began to have affairs. These were nothing serious until, in 1925, while in New York for a dinner with friends, she met Judd Gray, a thirty-three-year-old corset seller. His undistinguished appearance and weak personality seemed to be the exact opposite of Ruth's lively, feisty temperament. But, unexpectedly, there was a spark between them. For her, Gray was the perfect "love slave".

First there were fleeting meetings, then hours of passion. They saw each other at Ruth's house, when her husband was at work and her daughter was at school, or they arranged to meet in some hotel. Often Ruth took Lorraine with her to seem respectable, and left the little girl in the lobby to read or to play.

It was a short step for Ruth from adulteress to sly schemer.

Tough to Kill

Very soon, strange accidents began to happen to Albert Snyder. While he was changing the wheel on his Buick, he was nearly crushed under the car when the jack inexplicably slid away. He was locked in the garage and nearly suffocated by carbon monoxide from the car's engine; he was practically suffocated in bed by gas when Ruth went out for a walk, forgetting that the gas taps in the kitchen were open. He took an excessive dose of sleeping pills. While he was cleaning his boat, he bumped into his wife and fell overboard. After taking the "remedy" for hiccups, he became very ill.

Snyder does not seem to have suspected Ruth's murderous intentions. She even convinced him to sign a life insurance policy for $ 50.000 (which included a double indemnity clause in the event of a violent death) without creating any suspicions.

In 1927 Snyder was still obstinately alive, so Ruth decided to ask her lover boy for help.

A Truly Imperfect Murder

Judd Gray refused to kill Albert Snyder. But Ruth was relentless: she suggested, openly asked, flattered, and threatened. She repeated endlessly that they were made to be together, and for this reason they must get rid of her husband.

She was so insistent that Gray started drinking in excess, needing to calm his nerves. He tried to dissuade her, but in the end her power over him was enormous, and he gave in.

On the evening of May 19th, Gray went to Long Island to carry out a plan devised by Ruth. It was a cold, gray Saturday. He spent an hour wandering through the village, stopping from time to time to swig whisky from a flask, trying to pluck up his courage. Or, maybe, hoping to be seen: it was the middle of Prohibition, and if he had been arrested for drinking he would not have had to go through with the murder. But if this was what he wanted, it didn't work. Drunk, he entered the Snyder house and hid in an empty room, where he found three objects that he himself had obtained previously: a window counterweight, some wire and some chloroform. Ruth had said:

So we'll have three chances to kill him. One of them must work!

The family had gone to a party and didn't return before two. When the husband had gone to sleep, Ruth found Judd and led him into the bedroom. The two of them stood by the sides of the bed and she watched imperturbably as her lover struck Albert's head for the first time. It was not enough. Snyder woke up, cried out and grasped his aggressor, who was paralyzed with terror.

Help me Ruth!

both of them implored her. Quite calmly, Ruth took the weight from Judd, struck her husband more strongly, and neutralized him with the chloroform. Then she finished him off with the wire.

The couple staged a burglary. They turned the house upside down and Judd tied up Ruth. Then they parted. When Judd had gone, Ruth woke Lorraine and sent her to the neighbors' to ask for help.

Inspector George McLaughlin's detectives arrived quickly, but nothing in Mrs. Snyder's version was convincing: from the ropes that bound her, which were too loose, to her lack of injuries; from the excessive chaos, to the few signs of a break-in. Not to mention the imaginative description of the presumed burglar and murderer: "He was a big man with a thick black mustache, probably an Italian. Like Bartolomeo Vanzetti, the one in the Sacco and Vanzetti case."

When all the objects which, according to the woman's testimony, had been stolen were found inadequately hidden in the house, there were no more doubts. Surprisingly, Ruth gave in immediately. Less surprisingly, she accused Judd Gray of everything.

The latter was found hours later in a Syracuse hotel. He denied being in New York the evening before, forgetting that he'd thrown his train ticket in the waste basket of the room. And so, like Ruth, he accused his lover of everything.

Ruth Against Judd

The trial began on April 27th, 1927. Ruth was the first to take to the witness stand, entering a courtroom crowded with hundreds of spectators, journalists and celebrities of the time (among them was the director David W. Griffith, in search of inspiration). Those who could not be inside were able to hear the proceedings by means of microphones.

A PITILESS END

Nobody felt any compassion for Ruth Snyder. The press described her as a woman who was cold, calculating, heartless; they dubbed her variously as the woman of granite, the woman of marble, the vampire, the blond devil.
She was given no respect even in death: Thomas Howard, a journalist at the *New York Daily News*, strapped a hidden camera to his ankle and brought it to the execution, managing to capture on film the precise moment when the electricity surged into Ruth's body.The macabre image of the woman, bound to the electric chair with a black hood on her head, appeared on the front page the next day. So lasting was its fame that as late as 1991 Guns N' Roses, for the albums *Use Your Illusion*, were photographed posing in front of a giant reproduction of the image, with the banner headline *DEAD!* which appeared in the *Daily News* of the time.

Ruth played the part of a good mother, of a home-loving, church-going woman who was, above all, a neglected wife led astray by a depraved alcoholic lover who had forced her to get rid of her husband. Judd defended himself by maintaining that he had been seduced, manipulated, abused by a demon in female form, and that only she was guilty.

The jury believed both. After only thirteen days of trial, and an hour and a half of deliberation, Ruth and Judd were sentenced to the electric chair. The sentence was carried out on January 12th, 1928, in Sing Sing prison. The first to be executed was Judd Gray, who met his death calmly and quietly: "I'm ready," he said and smiled at the guards, "I have nothing to fear." A few minutes later, Ruth Snyder followed him. She took her leave of the world with these words:

Father, forgive them, they know not what they do.

Death of a Gigolo

Elvira Mullens Barney (United Kingdom)

It was 4.50 AM on May 31st, 1932, when Dr. Thomas Durrant was awakened in his London home by an excited telephone call. "Come quickly, doctor, there's been an accident." He rushed to the apartment of the wealthy Elvira Barney and found her sitting on the inner staircase embracing a young man. He had been shot by a pistol several times and killed. Had she killed him? Everything would suggest that this was so, but Elvira could count on the greatest lawyer of the day.

The young woman, practically naked, kept begging Dr. Durrant to save her lover. This was completely senseless, because the body of Michael Scott Stephen was clearly lifeless, having been killed by a Smith & Wesson .32 caliber pistol. The weapon had been left on the floor. When the police, led by inspector Alfred Campion, arrived, she was still undressed. In the sitting room there was a painting – which according to the police constables "would have been appropriate on the wall of a brothel in Pompei" – and around the house there was equipment for fetishist and sadomasochistic practices. When Campion asked her to put something on to accompany him to the police station, she burst out, "You don't want to put me in a cell, you filthy pig!" and, ignoring the inspector, telephoned her mother.

Elvira Barney, née Mullens, twenty-seven years of age, was the daughter of Sir John Ashley Mullens, a wealthy financier, and Lady Alexandra, a celebrity of fashionable London in the 1920s. The couple had had three daughters, but had always

Elvira Mullens Barney coming back home after her acquittal.

95

wanted a boy. The girls had been brought up with obsessively close attention by their mother, who controlled them to the point of suffocation.

Dangerous Liaisons

Probably for this reason, in adolescence Elvira turned into a rebel: she chose everything that might embarrass her noble family. To the point of deciding to marry, at twenty-three, John Sterling Barney, an American singer whom she had met at a party organized by her mother. John was part of the entertainment.

The marriage lasted only a few months, but it was violent. With John, Elvira began to use cocaine; and one day she showed a friend, Effie Leigh, the bruises and cigarette burns her husband had inflicted on her during sadomasochistic games. After the separation, Elivira continued to live a dissolute life thanks to the money he father gave her.

During a trip to Paris with Effie, Elvira met Michael Scott Stephen, who was three years younger than she was. His profession: to accompany rich women who were willing to maintain him and his passion for gambling. When they returned to London, they became lovers. She paid his debts and they organized parties together in the apartment at 21, Williams Mews, with drugs, drink, music, affairs and uncontrollable fights. When they were not at her home or at those of other young people in high society, they spent the night wandering between the *Café de Paris* and the other fashionable bars and restaurants.

A tragic fate was in store for the *Café de Paris* in London, where Elvira Barney had her last meal with Michael Scott Stephens, and where the scions of British high society tended to meet. It was a place of meetings and dinners, music, alcohol, and drugs. During the Second World War it was one of the few establishments which, thanks to friends in high places, was not closed.

"Under the dance floor there's an air raid shelter", assured the owners. But on the night of March 8th, 1941, a bomb from a plane fell on the café while Ken Johnson and his Orchestra were playing *Oh, Johnny*. It was a massacre. The *Café de Paris* only reopened in 1948.

Shots in the Night

In fact, Elvira and Michael spent their last night together at the *Café de Paris*. Then they returned to Williams Mews, where there was yet another fight. She later explained that she had not wanted to take part in the usual erotic games that he wanted, and that she had decided to leave him forever. She was tired of maintaining a man who, apart from everything else, was unfaithful to her. In fact, Elvira had discovered that Stephen went to gambling dens with another woman.

I can accept paying him, but not his girlfriend with whom he cheats on me. No way

she had confided to her friend Effie.

Neighbors related how that night, as often happened, they had heard cries and the noise of broken dishes.

We heard her shouting: I'll shoot you! I'll shoot you!

and immediately afterwards, the gunshots. Elvira maintained

that he had decided to kill himself and seized the pistol, and that she had tried to stop him, but that in the scuffle the gun had fired the two fatal shots.

The Importance of the Closing Argument

Sir John Mullens persuaded the best lawyer in England, Sir Patrick Hastings, to defend his daughter. "You cannot convict a young woman who still has all her life in front of her", he concluded, after having depicted the victim as an unfaithful rake who relied on his lover for everything.

The most brilliant closing argument that I have ever heard in my long court career.

Justice Humphreys said, explaining his decision to acquit the accused.

Sir Patrick, however, was wrong in predicting a long life for his client. In fact, Elvira, addicted to drugs, alcohol, and a rebellious life, died only four years later in Paris, where she never missed a chance to boast:

I'm the one who shot her lover.

The Girl in Yellow Pajamas

Linda Platt (Australia)

Australia, 1934. The partially burned body of a woman is found in a storm drain, wearing only yellow pajamas. It takes investigators ten years to identify it, and then only a few days to find the killer: her husband, an Italian waiter. Maybe this case will have to be reopened.

L inda Platt had always been restless. She was born in England in 1905, but emigrated first to New Zealand, and then to Australia. As a young woman, she was involved with some rather questionable characters. Then, in 1930, she married in Australia Antonio Agostini, a waiter from Treviso, Italy. He reported her missing at the end of August, 1934.

A week later, a certain Tom Griffith found the body of a woman in a storm drain that ran parallel to a road in Albury, halfway between Sydney and Melbourne. It was dressed in yellow silk pajamas, creased and singed from attempts to set fire to the body. There was no way to identify the victim. For the police it could just as easily be any other missing woman as Linda. While they waited for a break in the case, the body was kept in a formalin bath in the Department of Anatomy at the University of Sydney.

Ten Years Later

It was only in 1944 that new investigative techniques allowed the case to be reopened. According to the police, dental analysis showed that the victim was Linda Platt. Police commissioner

Linda Platt, later recognized as The Girl in Yellow Pajamas.

William MacKay found her husband and, in one way or another, convinced him to confess.

It was an accident. I didn't mean to kill her.

Agostini said, claiming that the gun had gone off by mistake, that he had panicked and, driven by fear, had tried to get rid of the body. Many people doubted this account. Linda was a good-looking woman. She had an alcohol problem, and she enjoyed the attention of men. Her jealous and possessive Italian husband had forced her to leave her friends in Sydney, and move to Melbourne. The court accepted Agostini's confession, however, and he was found guilty of culpable homicide. Without serving his full sentence, Agostini was released from prison in 1948, and he returned to Italy, where he died in 1969.

Unresolved Doubts

A killer who lucked out, then? Maybe not entirely. The case of the girl in yellow pajamas is still controversial, as not everyone is convinced by the official version. In 1944 the public image of the police needed improvement and Agostini – who might have had reasons not to protest – was perfect for the role of sacrificial victim. The Australian historian Richard Evans, in the well-documented book *The Pyjama Girl Mystery* published in 2004, claims even that the body that was found was not that of Linda Platt.

The Curse of Floreana

Eloise von Wagner Wehrborn (Ecuador)

On a desert island two men compete for the attention of an eccentric and domineering woman. Two other couples more or less in crisis complete the cast of this strange drama. Then one person disappears and another mysteriously dies. The puzzle might be impossible to solve.

Till 1932 only two families lived on the island of Floreana, in the Galapagos, a microcosm as beautiful as it was inhospitable. Friedrich Ritter and Dore Strauch had arrived from Berlin three years before, after abandoning their respective spouses. Friedrich was a doctor who was convinced that if he moved to an uncontaminated place, he could live to be a hundred. Dore had followed him, but their love dissipated soon after their arrival. She missed the Old Europe and the life she left behind.

Heinz and Margret Wittmer had chosen to live on Floreana to treat their ill son Harry with natural remedies. Margret was already pregnant and a few months later Rolf was born.

The two families tolerated each other but had no desire to go beyond the usual formalities. They survived on vegetables they grew, animals they raised, and gifts that infrequent tourists brought to the island.

When Eloise von Wagner Wehrborn landed on Floreana in September, 1932, accompanied by three men – two of whom were obviously her lovers – nobody could have foreseen how the delicate equilibrium on the peaceful island would be upset, or how all of them would soon slip into a deep abyss of suffering and mystery.

An Unusual Trio

Eloise was as determined as she was beautiful. She had used her charms to persuade Robert Philippson and Rudolf Lorenz to follow her to the ends of the earth:

> *I want to build a luxury hotel in the Galápagos. It will be called Hacienda Paradiso, and it will be magnificent!*

The enthusiasm of the "Baroness" (which was the title Eloise used to introduce herself) had infected even the government of Ecuador, who believed her plan would be good for the economy of the country.

Eloise had met Robert and Rudolf in Paris. The first was a German journalist, the second a penniless store owner. Soon both were inseparable from the woman.

Eloise easily convinced Rudolf to sell his store to finance the voyage to Floreana. It was more difficult for her to get him to

The "Baroness" Eloise von Wagner Wehrborn and her lovers: by her side, Robert Philippson and behind the two, Rudolf Lorenz.

accept that Robert would travel with them – together with Felipe Valdivieso, an unremarkable Ecuadorian destined to leave nothing behind for history.

Robert and Rudolf hated each other before long, but the woman was the one calling the shots. Robert may have played the part of the husband; on the other hand, Rudolf may have been the handyman of the band. He shied away and was always bossed around by both Eloise and Robert.

Rudolf lived only for Eloise: the more she mistreated him, the more he felt he could not live without her. From their first days on Floreana, he was forced to do the hardest work. Eloise very rarely had time for him, and he so suffered in silence. But just the hope of being able to spend a moment with his beloved was enough keep him going.

Relationships with the other inhabitants of Floreana were quickly soured by the bad behavior of the Baroness. Margret and Dore pitied Rudolf, who often sought them out: unable to break the irrational bond that tied him to his tormentor, the poor man still needed someone to talk to.

Vanished into Thin Air

As the months went by, Rudolf's health got worse: he realized that he would have to get away from Floreana and his unhealthy relationship. Eloise, however, was not prepared to accept this.

The situation was coming to a head. On March 19th, 1934, Dore helped Rudolf to prepare his departure. But in the following days the Baroness came to see him and he, predictably, couldn't refuse her.

On March 27th, Eloise decided to take the initiative and announced to all that she intended to leave on a cruise with Robert. She had grown tired of Floreana and wanted to move the hotel project to Tahiti. Rudolf was incredulous. In spite of death threats from Robert, he decided to go to the Hacienda to see his mistress one last time. Two days later he told the Wittmers that he hadn't been able to find either Eloise or Robert. Strangely, nobody had seen a boat tie up at Post Office Bay wharf, and of the two lovers there was no trace. They seemed to had vanished into thin air.

There was nothing more to keep Rudolf on Floreana and so, in mid-July, he abandoned the island.

Despite terrible conditions at sea, he convinced the owner of the boat to take him to San Cristobál, from where he could get to Guayaquil. In August, the inhabitants of Floreana were upset by news that the boat Rudolf had departed on never reached its destination.

An Open Ending

On November 20th, 1934, Friedrich died from food poisoning. Dore said that he had eaten spoiled meat. The fact that Friedrich was a committed vegetarian, added to the fact that Dore had recently been be-

MYSTERY AND PUBLICITY

Dore died in Berlin in 1942, Heinz in 1963. Margret, the last witness of these events, died in 2000, aged ninety-five. Children and grandchildren of the Wittmers still live on Floreana and manage a family hotel. The mystery of the island, which continues to inspire books and films (the latest, in 2013, *The Galapagos Affair: Satan Came to Eden* (2013), with Cate Blanchett), ensures its popularity and, perhaps, guarantees the success of its tourist activities.

having strangely, led Margret to suspect that she might have poisoned him.

Two days later, the body of Rudolf was discovered mummified by the sun on the island of Marchena. On December 7th, Dore, shaken by these events, left Floreana.

The series of disappearances and mysterious deaths that took place in 1934 remain unexplained today. According to many reconstructions, Rudolf killed Eloise and Robert, threw their bodies into the sea to be eaten by sharks, and then took excessive risks to escape the island.

Friedrich, in this account, helped Rudolf to complete the double murder, but this was discovered by Dore. She poisoned Friedrich because of the growing tensions in their relationship and perhaps because of her fear of meeting the same end as Eloise. Such speculation is destined to remain an untested hypothesis.

Love Takes Your Breath Away

Sada Abe (Japan)

Sada Abe, the "murderous geisha" of traditional Japan in the 1930s, represented the archetype of the woman castrator, a personification of one of the deepest-rooted nightmares in the male unconscious. At the time, her story attracted morbid attention. But years later it was re-interpreted as anticipating movements for women's rights.

I t had been her dream to become a geisha, an ethereal creature dedicated to the art of entertaining, a prestigious and much-desired role in Japan of the first decades of the twentieth century. The geisha possesses the grace and the rigorous discipline necessary to learn, and to pass on, traditional songs and dance. But Sada Abe, who grew up in Tokyo, was precociously independent, restless and rebellious: at fifteen years old she was raped, after which she led a wild and promiscuous life. Her father – it is not clear whether he did this to punish her or to meet her wishes – sold her to a geisha house in Yokohama. But Sada was too old to begin her apprenticeship as a geisha, and was assigned the more demeaning task of offering sexual satisfaction to clients of the house. These were the first steps down the road that would lead her into prostitution, first with a regular license, and later without it. In those years, her lovers were successful men, and she demonstrated a propensity for extreme sex.

Written on the Body

The word "love" was unknown to Sada until she met Kichizo Ishida. It was 1936 and the girl, who was then thirty, had decided to turn over a new leaf. She found work as a waitress in Tokyo, at the restaurant Ishida ran with his wife. The fact that Ishida was married did not prevent him from seducing the new waitress: in the spring of the same year the two were already lovers. When, on April 23th, they made a date in a tea house, the usual place for secret affairs, they had no idea what overwhelming passion lay in store. For the next four days, heedless of the visits of astonished maids, they staged an endless erotic encounter. They then left the place for another district, where their performance continued with alcohol and erotic games. It was two weeks later that they managed to disentangle. For Sada, it was a mystical experience, so absorbing that it made her dizzy. She was incapable of being apart from Ishida, and began to drink. The thought of having to share with another woman that body, that she felt belonged to her, was unbearable, and an obsessive idea formed in her befuddled mind:

If I killed him, no other woman could touch him.

Sada Abe's smile at the time of her arrest.

111

On their next date, the girl came armed with a kitchen knife. When they were naked, she lowered the knife to Ishida's genitals and warned her lover: she would deprive him of his virility, just to prevent him from enjoying himself with other women. Obviously the warning was only considered the outburst of a jealous woman. And those erotic games, which were so audacious – her hands around his neck at the moment of greatest pleasure, amplifying the orgasm again and again, and then her kimono belt in the same place, nearly choking him – seemed to him to be proof of an extraordinary harmony. He could not have imagined that they were actually taking part in the stage rehearsal for a personal ceremony: the one that Sada celebrated immediately after he'd gone to sleep. She tightened the cloth around his neck, until she was certain that he could no longer escape. Then she got ready to perform the most obscene rite: she brought the knife up to his lifeless body and did what she had threatened to do, slicing off her lover's genitals. She wrapped them carefully in paper and put them in her kimono. When interrogated about this gesture, she explained:

I wanted to take the part that aroused the most vivid memories in me.

Then she left the room, asking the maids not to disturb her sleeping companion.

One of the maids discovered the body on the morning of May 18th. It was clear what had happened and, so as not to leave any doubt, Sada had "signed" her action, writing in blood on the body, in delirious love, "Sada and Kichi together". Forever.

The "Panic of Sada Abe"

News of the case spread like wildfire, creating a sensation all over Japan. In various localities, sightings of the murderess

THE JURY WAS VERY MUCH INVOLVED

Japanese society of that time was extremely conservative and, although sexuality was apparently freer than elsewhere, people were reticent on some subjects. The uninhibited testimony of Sada Abe succeeded in involving and thrilling the nation, so much so that groups of women formed who were called "Sada fans". Even one of the three judges who dealt with the case admitted being excited by the spicy details of her account.

were reported, which caused scenes of chaos. And the government exploited the situation to distract public attention from what was, at the time, a period of political partisanship and difficulty.

Meanwhile, cooped up in her hotel room, Sada contemplated suicide. A few days later, she tried unsuccessfully to have sex with her lover's token, and then welcomed the arrival of the police with a smile. Her justification was simple:

I loved him so much. I wanted him all to myself.

She did not try to defend herself, but rather hoped for the death penalty. However, when she discovered that, among other things, she was accused of sexual perversion, Sada Abe fought for her dignity, to demonstrate that she was not depraved. The psychiatrists confirmed this: she was only a nymphomaniac.

The sentence was incredibly light: 6 years in prison for second degree murder. However, after 5 years an amnesty was proclaimed on the occasion of the 2600th anniversary of the first emperor Jinmu's coronation, and the woman was released. Although she then sought to live an anonymous, normal life, her story inspired many books and films and her figure became legendary.

The Beast
of Via San Gregorio

Rina Fort (Italy)

In November 1946, Milan was still recovering from the horrors of the war. It was accustomed to bloodshed. But the killing of a mother and her three children touched everyone. As told by Dino Buzzati in the *Corriere della Sera*, Rina Fort, a Friulan girl, had fallen in love with her employer, only to discover that he was married and the father of three children. When his wife arrived in the city from Catania with the children, Rina, her life marked by endless tragedies, slaughtered them all. But did she act alone?

The city was an accumulation of ruins. The air raids had hit the center as well as the outskirts, the Piazza Duomo, the factories, even the schools. Families struggled every day to find something to eat, to find something heavy to wear for the winter that had already arrived, to find firewood or coal for heating. But there was also, finally, the wish to begin anew, to throw themselves into various activities, and to plan for the future. This was what happened to Rina Fort, a young woman who arrived in Milan from Friuli to seek her fortune and escape a past marked by tragedy and misfortunes. Her father had died in an accident in the mountains, falling while trying to help her along a difficult path; and several relatives had had violent deaths, two committing suicide. Her first fiancée had died of tuberculosis only a few weeks before their wedding, and then she had discovered that she was sterile. At twenty-two she had married Giuseppe Benedet, a man from her town. On their wedding night he had dressed up

---

Rina Fort, the sole accused for the slaughter of Via San Gregorio.

as a woman, bound Rina and beaten her. In a matter of weeks she understood exactly what he was: completely crazy.

A Man All to Herself

To escape all this, in 1945 Rina Fort went to Milan and found a job as a clerk in a textile shop. The owner was Giuseppe "Pippo" Ricciardi, a Sicilian man who lived near the shop in Via San Gregorio 40, not far from Central Station. He lived alone. He was a good-looking man and, in a short time, the two became lovers. Indeed, in Rina's mind, she'd taken the first step to finally having the family she had always dreamed of. She had a man all to herself, and he was handsome and kind, and the owner of a store. And he was free. But free Giuseppe was not. He said nothing to his woman in Milan about having a wife, Franca Pappalardo (who was forty), and three children, Giuseppina, called Pinuccia (five), Giovannino (four), and Antonio (ten months) in Catania. To move in Italy in the immediate post-war period was very difficult and Giuseppe hoped that Franca would stay down in Sicily and be content with the letters that he sent her every now and then. After all, his wife had already been to Milan, but after some months she'd abandoned the foggy north for the sun of her Sicily.

Ricciardi very soon realized that he was falling in love with Rina. Indeed, he liked being with her in the store and at home. And even though they lived separate lives, their apartments were close. Furthermore, Rina had taken the reins of the business in hand, organizing things and correcting mistakes he made, which were serious enough to lead to its failure. But news travels fast, even in a country destroyed by war. Someone told Pappalardo that her husband in Milan had a steady lover. Franca, at that point, decided to leave Sicily: she would go to Giuseppe with their three children, resume her place at home, and put a stop to the moves of her dangerous competitor.

The Door is Opened to Horror

Rina Fort discovered the truth without warning. Not only that: it seemed that Franca was even expecting her fourth child. Giuseppe, driven by his wife and a sense of guilt, fired his loving store clerk and replaced her with another girl, Pina Somaschini. Then he left on a business trip to Prato, where the main textile factories were. The day Pippo was to return to Milan, the new clerk noticed that she didn't have her keys to open the shop. So early that morning she went to Via San Gregorio 40 to ask the wife of her boss to lend her the keys. She knocked, but there was no answer. Then she noticed that the door was not completely closed. She entered the apartment and beheld a scene of absolute horror. On the floor in a lake of blood and pieces of brain, she found Franca Pappalardo with her son Giovannino beside her, their heads smashed in with incredible violence. Pina screamed and sought help but did not enter a second room where, in a similar condition, there lay Pinuccia and, slumped in his highchair, little Antonio.

The first strange thing was that journalists and photographers arrived on the scene before the police. Who had told them? The second was that, when he returned from Prato, Giuseppe Ricciardi, on entering his apartment, first asked:

What has been stolen?

Rina Fort would confess that, to mislead the investigators, she had stolen some jewelry, throwing around drawers and linen.

But the first indication that the murder of the family was not a robbery that had ended badly, but had been motivated by jealousy, was that on the floor beside Franca's body investigators found a wedding photo of her with Pippo, torn into a thousand pieces. And in her hand, already stiff, the woman held a lock of black hair. On the floor beside the bodies and the pieces of the photo, there was also found a stylograph pen and a bunch of keys that belonged to neither Ricciardi, nor the killer. Was this a clue that there had been others involved in the slaughter?

On the other hand, it was not difficult for the investigators to find Rina Fort. Everyone knew of her relationship with Giuseppe and after a few hours commissioner Di Stefano went after her, first at her apartment, and then to the pastry shop where she had recently found a job. At police headquarters Fort first denied everything. Then, after an interrogation that lasted, without interruption, 17 hours – during which, she said, "they slapped me and one guy hit me with a club" – she began to confess. She admitted being the lover of her employer, and then told a story, variations of which would be retold during the trial. The last strange thing of those hours was that, when Ricciardi saw Fort at the police station, although by then he knew that she had killed his wife and children, he embraced her, saying:

My Rina, my Rina.

How Many Accomplices?

In her first confession to the commissioner, the woman explained that on the evening of November 29th she had gone to Franca to ask her to return to Catania: she wanted Giuseppe to be hers alone. The lady of the house offered her something to drink and said that it was up to her (Rina) to stand aside because Giuseppe had a family. Then jealousy got the better of her: Rina seized a metal bar that she found in the kitchen and hit her rival hard. Giovannino tried to defend his mother, but was in turn beaten to death. In her fury, Fort then also murdered Pinuccia and little Antonino.

Later, however, the woman told a different story, saying that

PEOPLE ARE AFRAID

Dino Buzzati was the *Corriere della Sera* journalist who followed the tragic "Beast of Via San Gregorio 40" case from the beginning. Here is an extract from his first article of December 3rd, 1946.

In the last few years people have had unparalleled training in the most imaginative spectacles of violent death and revenge – which, in spite of the age-old myths and the sad honor fables, is always one of the most abject sentiments. In recent years, the celebrated sacred rituals of incomparable power which have killed one, or two, or hundreds at a stroke, have really made the strengthened sensibility of our hearts waver. But this time the slaughter contains a dark improbability that evil, jealousy, greed, and meanness of spirit, all taken together, cannot explain. Only massacres by the furiously insane can approach such improbability. But was madness unchained in Via San Gregorio? Someone planned the slaughter, made an appointment, organized everything so that the alarm was not raised. Beyond the most unbridled perversity there always remained a wide margin of blood that no hatred could justify, thus altering the very measure of man, man, just as we've known him – with all his possible degradation – for centuries. Hence, fear. Someone else, different from us, was necessarily involved the other evening, a character of darkness, as found in a certain ancient history, the same character, perhaps, that for too long has infested our districts. And although until now he has made assignments without limits on our blood habits, this time he has overacted and given himself away. People are beginning to be afraid.

Pippo, who had gone to Prato only to construct an alibi, had sent her to the apartment. The initial idea had been to stage a robbery, to scare Franca and compel her to return to Catania; and by faking a robbery, the man would also have a reasonable excuse to avoid paying some heavy debts he had by then accumulated. Rina said that, on the instigation of her lover, she had met "with Carmelo, a Sicilian cousin or friend of Pippo who had given me a drugged cigarette. After smoking it I didn't understand anything anymore, I was just dazed."

According to this reconstruction of the event, Rina and Carmelo had gone to Via San Gregorio together. Franca had received them well, offering them a liqueur. And then the aggression had started. In court Fort added a new person, a mysterious second man who hit her with his fist on the nape of her head, knocking her out. She said:

I hit Franca, but I did not kill the children. It must have been Carmelo and the other man.

But who was Carmelo? The police finally identified him as Giu seppe Zappulla, a friend of Ricciardi's. At lineup, however, Rina Fort indicated the wrong person. Then, after some days, informed that her identification had failed, she asked if she could see the suspects again, and this time she indicated Zappulla, who was arrested with Pippo. The two men, although proclaiming their innocence, spent 18 months in San Vittore jail before being released. Zappulla died shortly afterwards from cancer. According to his relatives, however, he died because of the false accusation and the detention.

The trial began on January 10th, 1950. Pippo Ricciardi asked to be recognized as a plaintiff against Rina Fort. His brother-in-law attacked him fiercely:

You wretched husband and father, how dare you show your face at this trial!?

he screamed, and many inside and outside the court shouted against Pippo. However, since Ricciardi had been absolved of the accusations, he was admitted as an injured party.

The accused was present at all of the hearings, her face partially covered by a yellow scarf. For the press and public opinion she became the "Beast of Via San Gregorio 40". At the end, the jury found her guilty of the murders. She was condemned to life in prison, although her lawyer Antonio Marsico had tried in every way to show that the woman could not have acted alone that evening.

There were three glasses of the liqueur that Franca had offered on the table of the Ricciardi house. And who owned the stylograph pen and bunch of keys found beside the bodies?

The lawyer's questions remained unanswered. A psychiatric examination established that Rina was of totally sound mind, and therefore responsible for her actions. The sentence of life in prison was confirmed, and confirmed a second time on appeal.

Life Goes On

The "Beast of Via San Gregorio 40" served her sentence in various jails until the President of the Republic, Giovanni Leone, granted her a pardon in 1975. Out of prison, she took the surname of her husband, Benedet. She died a free woman on March 2nd, 1988.

Giuseppe Ricciardi remarried and with his new wife had a son. He died on September 12th, 1975, the same year Rina Fort was pardoned.

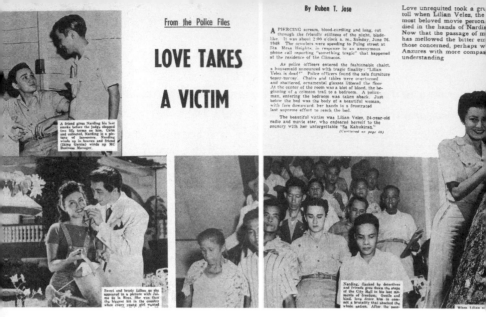

"Pop, Narding Has Killed Mom!"

Lilian Vélez (Philippines)

Everyone in the Philippines knew her bright, smiling face, her long jet-black hair. For this reason, the public was profoundly upset when the newspapers reported the murder of the young actress and singer Lilian Vélez and her governess Pacita. In the villa of Lilian, little Vivian was still holding her mother's death-cold hand when, in Quezon City, the first details of the murder began to circulate.

They were years of confusion, conflicts, dreams, hopes, the years following the intense period of struggle for independence in the Philippines. The United States had relaxed its control but its influence continued to weigh heavily. Tired of typhoons, earthquakes, floods, and wars, the people sought consolation in the dazzling illusions of the cinema, which in the 1930s had begun to appeal to all social strata thanks to the release of the first

films in Tagalog. The lives of the stars were followed with growing interest. Thus when, on June 26th, 1948, the actress Lilian
Vélez (twenty-four) met her death at the hands of her screen
partner, Bernard Narding Anzures, the whole archipelago was
plunged into mourning.

The Accursed Break-in

It happened at night, while the house was wrapped in silence.
Someone was knocking at the door. First softly, then more in-
sistently, furiously. Lilian's governesses, Pacita and Nenita, got
up to open the door, but the young woman stopped them. She
knew that behind the door a man was waiting, a man furious with
blind, violent passion. The sound of breaking glass startled her.
Decisively, Lilian ordered Nenita to take Vivian into the bedroom and lock the door. Then she went into the sitting room,
ready to meet her fate. Bernardo Anzures stood there, in front of
her. The man tried to grab her, and a desperate struggle ensued:
chairs and tables were upset, and everywhere ceramics and crystal
shattered into thousands of pieces. Lilian tried to run away, but
she tripped. Anzures, at her back, brandished a knife: he stabbed
her with all his strength and killed her. Then he gave vent to his
murderous fury on Pacita, and fled. He could not accept the fact
that Lilian Vélez had a new screen partner, Jaime de Rosa. He was
crazy with rage.

A few hours later, Joe Climaco, Lilian's husband and manager,
returned home. There to meet him was little Vivian, beside herself:

Pop, Narding has killed Mom!

The next morning, Bernard Anzures was arrested and sentenced to life in prison, but pardoned by President Elpidio Quiri-
no. Two months after his release, however, he died of tuberculosis.

---

*Top left: Narding Anzures waiting for the verdict; below: Lilian and Jaime de Rosa; in the
middle: Narding's last moments of freedom before the jail.*

Under the White Ermine

Pia Bellentani (Italy)

It is the evening of September 15th. At Villa d'Este, on Lake Como, an exclusive show of fashion, music and dance is in progress, glasses full of *spumante*. The wealthy, postwar middle class have come together for a fashionable evening. In silk and chiffon, among smiles and gossip, this drama of jealousy quickly approaches the tragic end of romantic love.

The white satin dress hugged her hips, with silver sequins shining in its folds. Supported by a single crossed strap around her neck, it left the Countess's shoulders bare. She'd, in fact, deposited her ermine cape in the cloakroom of the Grand Hotel di Villa d'Este, in Cernobbio.

Pia Bellentani, the wife of Count Lamberto, had been unsure until the last moment, undecided about whether to take part in the party. She'd been forced to take to her bed in the previous hours, when a phone call from Lilian Sacchi had woken her and persuaded her to prepare. Without thinking about it too much, she put on that pure white dress and a diamond necklace that lit up her neckline. Her face, however, remained dark as, deep in thought, she stared into space.

Count Bellentani, under a yellow cashmere pullover, had decided to bring his .9 Browning Fegyvergyar, a Hungarian-made pistol, to protect his wife, the jewels, and the fur. This was almost a habit, as it was for many in those times – after all, he had never used the old revolver. It had been three years since the end

---

The Countess Pia Bellentani escorted by her brother Giulio during the days of the trial.

of the Second World War. But it was only a few months ago that the new government was elected, with the Christian Democrats almost reaching an absolute majority. The new rich middle class and aristocratic families could finally sleep soundly at night.

An Exclusive Party

You could feel the crisp air of the mid-September evening: it was enough to leave ajar the great glass windows of the *sala delle Colonne* to feel it on the skin. The still, dark waters of Lake Como reflected the crystal chandeliers of one of the finest hotels in Europe, and absorbed its fashionable chat interspersed with notes from a small orchestra. On a runway in the center of the hall Biki's high fashion was on display by haughty young models in high heels. It was the Milanese stylist who organized the party on the lake: the new fall/winter 1948/49 collection was ready. All the people who counted in high society sat at the tables at the edge of the red carpet, smiling pleasantly and making small talk. Among those present were Baron Rothschild and his wife; Sabry Pascià, the uncle of the Egyptian King Faruq; the industrialist Leopoldo Surr and his wife, the Locatellis, and the fashion journalist Elsa Haertter. A perfect setting for the spectacle that was about to begin.

The hours, like the dancers on the marble floor and the beautiful women twirling silk and organza, slid by, careless and bored. There was tension at the Bellentanis' table. Opposite Pia sat Carlo Sacchi, her lover, a Milanese industrialist made rich by textiles; next to him sat his wife, Lilian, a friend of Pia's, who had been a dancer in the Viennese theaters. Pia and Carlo's affair had been going on for more than three years, but it had now come to an end. The respective spouses apparently knew nothing. But in reality they knew everything, and said nothing for the sake of a quiet life. A little further on, at another table, sat Mimì Cozzi, Carlo's new lover, already negotiating a divorce from her husband.

As at every party, frequent invitations to dance mixed up the seating arrangements. Pia had been asked several times, but had politely refused, glacial, distant, with her fingers interlocked and her elbows on the table, weighing up how much loneliness and bitterness she felt in that din. The words exchanged with Carlo that evening had been fleeting and excruciating – in private he rejected her but in public he wanted to waltz: "You won't dance with me because you're not excited," he said sententiously, adding, his face hard: "Even if you don't come with me, your husband is destined to be a cuckold." He could no longer stand her extreme and intrusive love, and she could not accept rejection, the coarseness and arrogance of the man she believed she loved.

The Inevitable Happened

Shortly after half past one, a shot was heard amid the clamor of the last waltzes, but at first no one realized what had happened. Carlo Sacchi thudded to the floor, his hand to his chest, a grimace frozen on his face the moment the bullet pierced his heart. A few steps way stood Pia, a smoking revolver in her hand, on her shoulders the ermine stole which had hidden the weapon. She'd personally collected both items from the cloakroom.

A silent shudder, and the frenzy of desperation: the Countess pointed the weapon at her temple and tried to fire again, but the pistol did not go off.

It won't fire! It won't fire any more!

she screamed, and an instant later the pistol was wrested from her hands, and someone slapped her twice, to get her out of shock.

The last conversation between the two lovers had been harrowing: "Well, what's happening?" Carlo had asked her near the bar. "What's happening is that it's over, really over," she had answered, looking him straight in the eye. In the moment that she pronounced this sentence she felt the ridiculousness of already said words. So she tried again: "I mean that I can kill you. I have a pistol here". This was snubbed by another arrogant reply:

The usual comic strip novels. The usual Southern blusterers.

The pistol shot inevitably followed, without intention and without taking aim, Countess Bellentani would later say. In the hall, there was restrained, elegantly irrational excitement. Biki's husband, the Frenchman Roberto Bouyeure, sighed:

Ah, les italiens!

The drama was concluded, and Pia fell exhausted into a chair.

Daughter, Wife, Lover

Pia Caroselli did not belong to that world. She entered it as an adult, through the ambition of her mother, Nazarena, who wanted to "set her up" with a rich man and a position in society. She had grown up in Sulmona, surrounded by the Abruzzo peaks. Her father, Romeo, was a building contractor who in those years made a fortune. She was educated in an excellent convent school in Rome, studying literature, playing the piano, and writing poetry. She had a particularly sensitive, reserved, and melancholy soul, and was obsessed by death. She suffered from an "existential malaise" that made her reject the world. At twenty, she seemed to have fallen in love, but with the wrong person (for her family): he was only a provincial lawyer, not good enough for the daughter of the Carosellis.

Her mother took her on vacation to Cortina d'Ampezzo, but she avoided the glances of the men who threw themselves at her feet, enchanted by her dark hair, her light eyes, her statuesque body. Count Lamberto Bellentani of Reggio Emilia, the owner of a cured meats company, noticed her, and stubbornly found a way of seeing her through a friend of Sulmona's who turned out to be an uncle of the girl's. He courted her and shortly afterward married her in Milan, on July 15th, 1938.

She was twenty-two years old and Lamberto was thirty-nine, but he always tried to reduce this gap with special attention, with comforts, with the luxuries that the girl's mother had hoped she would have. In the early years, they lived in Reggio Emilia, and their villa was often alive with light for their dearest friends and the most important families. Pia seemed happy: perhaps she was living the best years of her life. Stefania and Flavia were born, one year apart, and both times she hoped it would be a boy. That strange melancholy remained in the recesses of her soul.

When the war began, the Bellentanis moved to Cernobbio, on the lake, where the fashionable life became more intense. They were sheltered: tragedy did not touch them. In 1940, among the stuccoed arches of the Hotel des Bains at the Lido di Venezia, they made the acquaintance of the Sacchis and their three daughters. There was no spark, no lightning between Pia and Carlo; first they were acquaintances, then they were friends, and the families began to see each other. She struck up a friendship with Ada Mantero Locatelli, Carlo's sister, who considered her brother "an intelligent man, but insensitive, chronically cynical."

The event which totally upset this stability was the death of Silvia, Carlo's eldest daughter. He needed to be consoled, she chose to take care of him, and she discovered another man; he let himself fall into her arms, and she hoped to make a better man of him. They became lovers, and they heedlessly allowed themselves be seen together.

But within a year, Carlo grew tired of her, the game no longer amusing to him – he already had too many lovers. She went out of her mind with jealousy: she could not give up the man who had made her heart beat for the first time. She tried to kill herself by throwing herself under his car. She wanted him to be part of her life, for good or ill. Their affair was over, and he was already being seen hand in hand with another woman, Mimì.

By then he was deriding her, avoiding her, condescending to her. But the Countess could not let go, she had no one to fall back on, and a few days before that September 15th she sank into despair.

The Trial in Court and in the Media

The Bellentani case filled the newspaper front pages for weeks: in that gilded world, among "respectable people", adultery and jealousy, blood and death had been intertwined. With the end of the war, Fascist censorship of the news had also ended: the events of Villa d'Este could not have been juicier.

Famous journalists, from Vitaliano Brancati to Camilla Cederna, wrote editorials; and the various accounts were detailed, written by many who unexpectedly found themselves special correspondents. By leafing through *Epoca*, *l'Unità*, *Tempo illustrato*, one could also see the black and white photographs of the gala evening.

Basically, the story was commonplace: they were having an affair and, gripped by jealousy, she had slain him with her husband's pistol. It was witnessed by dozens of people.

But public opinion was divided. Some played down the Countess' guilt, considering her a victim: she had loved too much, she had been unfaithful to her husband with her only love, and she had hopelessly lost control. But some considered her corrupt and as guilty as Carlo: she had given in to an adul-

A STORY OF LOVE AND DEATH

In her support, the defense argued that there was a lack of intention to commit the murder. While the crime was certainly carried out, it was done without planning. And there were Sacchi's continual provocations: Pia was exasperated by Carlo's insulting demeanor.

The psychiatric examination was done by professor Filippo Saporito, whose findings, reported in more than 600 pages, attested to Pia's total mental infirmity.

However, no doubts were ever advanced about the intention to commit the crime. After In Pia's first words at the time of the murder, when in a state of shock she had tried to maintain that it was an accident, that the loaded pistol had been fired by mistake, the accused admitted that she had pressed the trigger knowingly, albeit only to frighten her lover.

Immediately on realizing that she had killed Sacchi, she had tried to end it all by making the ultimate sacrifice, to put an end to her suffering and to avoid the consequences of the act. Some said that if she had succeeded, hers would simply have been "a story of love and death". The jammed the pistol, which was old and rusty for lack of use, prevented her suicide and forced her to look reality in the face.

terer's flattery and was tainted with the same vices, with no extenuating circumstances.

The woman was defended by the attorney Angelo Luzzani, who tried to play the card of unfitness to plead: Pia Caroselli Bellentani had always been a fragile, excessively emotional woman, "with phases of over-excitement and depression with a melanchonic basis", as we read in the proceedings. Several times she had attempted suicide. Her amorous passion for Carlo Sacchi had progressively aggravated the "morbid process".

However, the Countess was never able to admit her adulterous relationship. She justified it to herself with an idealistic purpose: to redeem a cynic, to enable him to regain confidence in himself and faith in God. When she discovered that he had had other, ongoing relationships, she finally collapsed. She allowed herself to be humiliated, and became dominated by the situation. Before taking part in that last gala, she wrote to him:

> Carlo, I don't reproach you, believe me. I blame everything on the hardness of life. If you don't love me, it's not your fault, and I can't stop loving you because of this. But, oh God, why do I have to torment myself so much, to suffer in this way?

Her decline reached its nadir that evening at the Villa d'Este, when she saw him side by side with his new lover.

The verdict was pronounced on March 12th, 1952. Pia Bellentani was found to be partially mentally infirm and was sentenced to 10 years for the voluntary manslaughter of Carlo Sacchi, 3 of which were to be served in an institution. On appeal, the sentence was reduced to 7 years and 10 months. She was transferred from the prison in Como to the hospitals for the criminally insane in Aversa and then in Pozzuoli.

On December 23rd, 1955, the President of the Republic, Giovanni Gronchi, pardoned her. Shortly after her release, her husband Lamberto, who had moved to Montecarlo, died. Pia settled in Rome with her daughters, and took up her role of mother again. She lived the last years of her life in quiet privacy.

The Truth of Pauline

Pauline Dubuisson (France)

Despite the bigoted morals of the post-war years, Pauline Dubuisson always got everything she wanted, boys included. Presumptuous as much as she was fragile, at twenty-four she had still not learned to accept refusal; nor, perhaps, to recognize love. For this she could not forgive Félix, the fiancée who abandoned her for another woman.

What happened on March 17th, 1951, was the most dramatic action of a story that had begun many years before in Malo-les-Bains, a small village in the north of France. Pauline Dubuisson, the third child of a well-off family was born there on March 11th, 1927. Her father André was an authoritarian head of the family: he believed in the value of discipline and thought he should give his daughter a rigid upbringing. He wanted her to face the world with her head held high. Her mother Simone, on the other hand, was an ordinary woman, without emotional hang-ups and completely submissive to the figure of her husband, ful-ly respecting the good bourgeois norms of the age. It was in this austere atmosphere that the character of Pauline grew up, devel-oping a mixture of stubborn arrogance, pride and opportunism.

The girl's adolescence coincided with the Second World War and was seriously affected by it: the conflict overwhelmed the Dubuisson family and Pauline, because of her good looks and desire to experience new things, ended up taking a German officer as a lover. She was accused of collaboration at the end of the war. Although her youth, together with the providen-tial intervention of her father, saved her from being sentenced, in the country village gossip was divided between those who considered her an informer, or traitor, and those who resorted to much more vulgar terms. To Pauline, all this mattered lit-tle. The throne of presumption from which she observed others was too high for their judgment to worry her. Nevertheless, she knew she would have to put the situation behind her in order to begin anew. Thus, when she was eighteen, she moved to Lyons, where she lived with an aunt, and a little later moved to Lille, where she began to attend the Faculty of Medicine.

A Tormented Relationship

In the course of her first year Pauline dedicated herself to boys as much as she did to her studies, collecting a thick portfolio of lov-ers with which she had intense but fleeting affairs, every relation lacking in feeling but loaded with passion. She met Félix in the autumn of 1947, during a lesson, and Pauline quickly realized

Pauline Dubuisson's haughty expression during the trial.

that with him things would be different: the young man did not want a banal adventure but something much more committed. Despite the little affinity he felt for her, Félix was strangely intrigued by this young person, with her thoughtful ways and mild temperament, whose fragile emotionality seemed to contrast with her sturdy physique. The engagement between the two soon became official and for some time things seemed to work. Soon enough, the girl was introduced to the Bailly family.

But behind her thick black hair, the sweet blue eyes and the romantic attitudes that had bewitched the young man, there lurked a woman of a very different nature, one who was amused by playing the part of the model fiancée but who, deep down, considered Félix on a par with the many other men she had had in the past. She also didn't feel any love for him. When the young man talked of getting married, Pauline realized that the time had come to end the charade. The girl knew well how to hurt the sensitive mind of her fiancée and so, partly through boredom and a little out of spite towards that sentimentality that she could not share, she began, in playing view of her fiancée, going around with other men. Félix got tired of that very quickly, and in the summer of 1949 their engagement was basically over.

The young man moved to Paris in order to forget Pauline and to continue with his studies. The affair did not seem to have any effect on Pauline, but when in the spring of 1951 she heard that Félix was close to marrying, the woman felt confused and upset. In the preceding months she had often thought of him but her arrogant soul had prevented her from accepting the idea that she needed Félix, that the emptiness that she felt was due to his absence, or that she might have fallen in love with him. With news of the engagement, then, she knew she had to do something and do it soon. So on March 6th she left for Paris, determined to resume her relationship with her former fiancée.

Crime and Punishment

Félix had an apartment at number 25 of Rue de la Croix Nivert and it was there that Pauline presented herself the evening of her arrival. The disheartened face, the disconsolate voice and the imploring ways got her into the apartment without too much difficulty. A little surprised and a little scared, the young man was struck by her unexpected visit, and the two ended up spending the night together. But the following morning Pauline was dismissed without hesitation: however much he had been shaken for the night before, Félix did not want to give her a second chance. He considered their affair over, and he intended to marry just as he had planned. Pauline had never considered the possibility of being rejected by Félix, who one time had faithfully loved her; suddenly their roles seemed to be reversed, and Pauline's pride found this unacceptable. Having exhausted her entreaties, in the following days she moved on to threats, to the extent that Félix's friends, worried about him, decided to organize guard shifts, in order to not leave the young man alone.

On the morning of March 17th, Pauline knocked on Félix's door again, asking to speak to him in private. Félix preferred to give her appointment in the nearby Place Cambronne, a crowded place where he would feel more at ease. Pauline agreed to this, but she did not turn up for the meeting; later on it would transpire that she had hidden in a nearby bar in order to watch Félix and to wait for him to return home, so that she could follow him. When she showed up at the apartment again, the young man found himself alone: Bernard, the friend who should have been there, was late. Confronted by the sad and petitioning face of the woman, Félix surrendered and decided to let her in.

In a matter of minutes the two found themselves arguing furiously until Pauline, overcome by anger and lost clarity of thought, pulled out a gun and fired three shots at Félix, two of which hit him in the head. The obsession for the young person had lead her to a point of no return: what would she do now? How would she go on? Upset, she decided to take her own life. When Bernard reached the apartment he found it full of gas, with Félix in a pool of blood and Pauline unconscious on the floor. He succeeded in saving the woman but by now there was nothing that could be done for his friend.

The French press was interested in the case immediately and found it easy to arouse the morbid curiosity of the public, to the extent that on the day the trial began, the court was packed with people who wanted to see Pauline and to hear what she had to say. But most of their expectations were disappointed: in the dock there was no diabolic *femme fatal* but only a slight and innocuous woman who maintained a fierce detachment for the entire trial in spite of the serious words of accusation and the extensive testimony given against her. The verdict surprised nobody: guilty of homicide that was not premeditated. The sentence was life in prison. It was an exemplary sentence that the girl served in an equally exemplary way, until she was released for good behavior in 1959.

Some time later she changed her name to Andrée and moved to Morocco, where she hoped to start a new life. Here the Fates seemed finally to smile on her: she found a good job and met a

THE TRUTH, A FILM ON PAULINE

In 1960 *The Truth*, directed from Henri-Georges Clouzot and starring Brigitte Bardot, was released in France. Although the characters in the story have different names, the plot clearly follows the vicissitudes of Pauline and Félix's relationship: the young Dominique, in the film, is accused of murdering her fiancée, Gilbert. Taking her side, the story is told through flashbacks that piece together the youth of the girl, her troubled history of love, her education, and victimization by the hypocrisy of modern society. The film was an immediate success and was nominated for best foreign film of the year at the Oscars. At the same time, *The Truth* brought Pauline back under public scrutiny, and pushed the woman to leave France for Morocco.

forty-year-old engineer, Maurice, who fell in love with her and asked her to marry him. Sure of Maurice's love for her, one night the woman decided to lift the weight and reveal her troubled past. But the reaction of the man was of dismay and disgust, and the next morning Pauline found herself abandoned. She felt betrayed and humiliated. The world collapsed around her, and just when she had tried to be honest with the one she loved. It was with these bitter thoughts that, on a warm day in September, 1963, she killed herself with barbiturates. The cold solitude that had accompanied her all her life enfolded her for the last time, and Pauline sank into a sleep without dreams or regrets.

Victim and Executioner

Pierre and Yvonne Chevallier (France)

Four shots hit home: one in the chest, one in the forearm, one in the thigh and one in the chin. Little Mathieu rushed in, scared by the sound of the gunfire, and saw his father lying in a pool of blood. Yvonne, perfectly calm, led him downstairs and left him with the maid. Then she returned to the room, with the body of Pierre almost lifeless on the ground, and fired a last shot. She waited a moment before calling the police: "My husband needs you urgently." On the arrival of the police she was already dressed in mourning and, without objection, she followed them through a crowd that was calling for her death.

Pierre Chevallier, of an illustrious Orléans family, was a young man full of promise. In 1937, when he was still studying medicine, he met Yvonne Rousseau, a timid nurse of humble origins. Brought up on a small farm, she was a total stranger to Pierre's cultured and refined world and, as in the most predictable of scripts, she was an easy conquest. Swept up by unrestrainable passion, the young man and woman shortly found themselves married. But many more significant events were happening in those years: for Pierre, soon to become the father of Mathieu, the war was the chance to prove his courage and patriotism. He enlisted as a volunteer in 1940 in the Free French, followers of Charles de Gaulle, and saw action in the ranks of the Resistance. By the end of the conflict, he was a war hero. Awarded the Legion of Honour, he set out on a political career and was elected mayor of Orléans.

An Embarrassing Wife

Pierre quickly found himself in his element, in his new role as a public figure. He began to travel to Paris and spend time there for official meetings and formal dinners. But under the pitiless floodlights of the bourgeois salons, the hopeless social inadequacy of his wife became plain.

Yvonne, who in the meantime, had given birth to their second child, was awkward, drab, incapable of behaving correctly in society, and she couldn't hold an intelligent conversation. Yvonne had unconditional admiration for her husband. Thus Pierre's progressive loss of interest in her was dramatic and lacerating. The more his Parisian visits were prolonged, the more Yvonne became disheartened, and she slipped into an abyss of depression. When Pierre returned he did not hide his intolerance, remaining closed to the attempts of his wife to attract a look: if not his affection, at least some compassion. Yvonne tried to overcome her deficiencies by reading widely and looking after her appearance, but Pierre's

Yvonne Rousseau at the time of her acquittal (on the left). She had been accused of the murder of the husband, Pierre Chevallier (on the right).

contempt and coldness was brutal. After yet another act of supplication, he exploded: "Find yourself a lover! You disgust me."

Love Letters

It was by now evident that Pierre's attentions were directed elsewhere, but it was an anonymous letter which accused him of betrayal. Yvonne then went through her husband's things and found what in her heart she would have preferred not to find. Words written on paper, as brazen in their eloquence as in their signature: Jeannette.

Jeanne Perreau was her attractive neighbor, younger, more beautiful, and more sophisticated. Her husband Léon owned one of most prestigious department stores in the city, but he seemed unconcerned about the reputation his red-haired Jeanne had acquired as a seductress. Yvonne believed she was entitled to some respect as a wife, and went to Paris to demand it. Instead, she met with further humiliation: she was refused entry by a porter on the express instruction of her husband, and had to return home without seeing him. On his return Pierre did not show any remorse, claiming that the matter had nothing to do with him. Yvonne cried, shouted at him, and tried to commit suicide. Then she got a permit to carry a gun. She bought a MAB .7.65mm pistol.

A Crime of Passion

11 August, 1951. Pierre, recently announced secretary to the Minister of Education, was preparing for his inauguration ceremony. He looked with satisfaction at his image in the mirror. Yvonne came in with the same imploring look as always, but for him she was nothing but a burden. The word "divorce" re-echoed through

the room like a bomb. The woman, beside herself, raced to the cupboard and extracted the pistol. With thin hands, and sunken eyes, Yvonne aimed the weapon at herself, determined to end it.

If you leave me, I'll kill myself!

When Pierre answered pitilessly, "Kill yourself. It would be the best thing you ever did", something in her rebelled, and rather than shoot herself she turned the gun on the man she loved so much.

Although initially the sentence for the killer of a war hero seemed a foregone conclusion, the story of Yvonne and her suffering, so in contrast with the effrontery of Jeanne, won the sympathy of the public and the Court. The judge reproached her in a paternal way, while she repeated: "I'm sorry, I'm sorry" over and over again. In response to the crowd shouting "Free her!" the jury found Yvonne "Not guilty".

In those days, the French criminal code accepted a crime of passion as attenuating guilt, no doubt born of the need to pardon men who committed murder on finding their wives in flagrant acts of adultery. This was one of the rare cases in which the norm was applied in reverse, in favor of the woman.

SELF-INFLICTED PUNISHMENT

The case of Yvonne Chevallier attracted enormous media interest. Various writers saw it as emblematic of the feminist struggle. The name Yvonne became known all over the world as someone who is the victim of a crime of passion.
Although acquitted by the State and the Church, the woman felt remorse and a growing sense of guilt. Unable to live with such a past, she decided to start over and spent her remaining years helping others, as a missionary nurse. She died quietly at seventy-two.

Who Killed Marilyn Sheppard?

Sam Sheppard (United States)

Kokie, the family's little dog, did not bark on the night of July 4th, 1954, when Marilyn Reese Sheppard, a woman of thirty-one years in her fourth month of pregnancy, was brutally killed in the bedroom of her home in the suburbs of Cleveland, Ohio. Her husband, Dr. Sam Sheppard, brusquely woken by the woman's cries, stated that he saw an intruder with "bushy" hair run off. The police did not believe him. Thus began one of the longest, and most controversial, unresolved criminal cases in American history. As Ernest Hemingway said: "A trial like this, with its elements of doubt, is the most exciting of human stories."

M r. and Mrs. Sheppard spent the eve of the holiday, July 3rd, dining with their neighbors, Don and Nancy Ahern, and their respective children. From the patio of the comfortable home in the Bay View neighborhood they could see the moon mirrored in Lake Erie. Marilyn and the Aherns stayed up late watching the film *Strange Holiday*, while Sam, after a shift in the operating room, dozed on the divan. The day was ending in the best possible way and there was no hint of the horror to come.

Sam and Marilyn had met in high school in Cleveland. Attracted by the handsome young man and his undeniable sporting and academic talents, the girl married him in 1945, in Los Angeles, where her new husband was completing his residency in neurosurgery. When they returned to Ohio, Sam began his career working with his brothers Stephen and Richard, in the

Sam Sheppard's imprisonment: he will serve a life sentence.

clinic founded by their father in Bay View. That evening, Marilyn's last, the couple announced the end of a crisis in their marriage and the coming birth of their second child.

The Murder and the First Trial

There was blood everywhere in the bedroom, and Marilyn's face was unrecognizable. While she was raped and struck 27 times, her son Sam "Chip" was asleep in the next room but didn't hear anything. Her husband found her semi-naked, her skull crushed to pulp. Somebody had just killed her and then staged a burglary. That "somebody" then also threw himself on Sam.

Sam Sheppard was admitted to hospital, where, officially, he was still innocent. But then the other woman showed up. Mr. Sheppard denied everything, but Susan Hayes, interrogated by the police, admitted the affair.

On July 30th the *Cleveland Press* came out with a front page headline: "Why isn't Sam Sheppard in prison?" That evening, the husband was arrested and charged with first-degree murder. The case not only caused intense excitement in the peaceful Ohio town, but crossed state lines and soon became a national obsession. Over the years, many books examining the crime were published, and the television series *The Fugitive*, inspired by Sam's story, was an unprecedented success. The vehemence of the press oriented public opinion; later, it would even be accused of prejudice against the doctor, since it had immediately considered him the only suspect.

The trial opened on October 18th. On December 21st the jury pronounced the guilty verdict: second-degree murder. Sheppard was sentenced to life in prison. After his conviction, his mother,

Ethel, took her own life, and his father died of a gastrointestinal hemorrhage provoked by stomach cancer. In 1963 Marilyn's father, Thomas S. Reese, committed suicide in a hotel room.

New Evidence

The doctor's attorney, William Corrigan, made every effort to obtain an appeal, but without success. In 1955 he hired the criminologist Paul Leland Kirk. Kirk, examining traces of blood left at the crime scene, demonstrated both that a third person had been present and that the crime had been committed by a left-handed person, effectively excluding Dr. Sheppard. A few years later, this evidence would prove crucial.

In November, 1959, the window washer Richard Eberling was arrested for burglary. Among the objects in his possession was a ring belonging to Marilyn Sheppard. When he was interrogated by the police, he stated that he had washed the windows of the Sheppard home a few days before the crime. He added that on that occasion he had also lost blood from a cut on his finger. With Eberling, there emerged a possible murderer, perhaps the famous man with the "bushy" hair.

The Intervention of the Supreme Court

In July, 1964, after ten years in prison, Sheppard was finally released on the order of a district court, because he had not received a fair trial due to the interference of the media.

The involvement of the Supreme Court, which was called upon to listen to the arguments of the State of Ohio and Sheppard's attorney, made this case a milestone in balancing the rights of the press and those of the citizen.

CONSTITUTIONAL CONFLICTS

The Sheppard case opened a constitutional conflict between the First Amendment of the Constitution of the United States, which guarantees the freedom of the press, and the Sixth Amendment, which assures every citizen a fair trial and an impartial jury. In ensuring a fair trial, what is the margin of intervention for a judge or a court under the First Amendment? In this case, the Court considered, for example, the distance between the press table and the jury bench: it was less than three feet. The journalists' closeness to the trial participants was considered detrimental to the privacy between Sheppard and his attorney.

The Supreme Court declared a mistrial, citing the "carnival" atmosphere that had surrounded it and "the chaos reigning in the courtroom".

On October 24th, 1966, the second trial of Sam Sheppard began. Media access was regulated and the jury was forbidden to make contacts outside. This time the doctor was acquitted: no evidence linked him to his wife's murder. Sam was a free man, but his life was now haunted by ghosts of the past. He decided to take up medicine again, but failed miserably after causing the death of two of his patients during operations. Ostracized by his son and his brothers, he would also eventually divorce Arianne Tebbenjohanns, the woman he had met during his time in prison and had married as soon as he was released.

In 1970, at the age of forty-six, Sam Sheppard died of alcohol abuse. Shortly before his death, he married Colleen Strickland, the daughter of the professional wrestler George Strickland, and had debuted as a wrestler under the stage name of Killer Sheppard.

An Endless Case

Sam Sheppard's body was exhumed in 1997 to perform a DNA test, but no evidence of guilt emerged. Richard Eberling remained the primary suspect. While he knew the Sheppards' house well, and some blood at the scene of the crime was certainly his, his presence at the moment of the murder could never be demonstrated beyond any doubt.

On February 14th, 2000, Sam Reese Sheppard, Sam and Marilyn Sheppard's son, sued the State of Ohio for wrongful imprisonment: he demanded $ 2 million in damages and the restoration of his father's reputation. The verdict was the "non-innocence" of Dr. Sheppard in his wife's death.

Although this trial ended almost 50 years after the horrendous crime, the question still remains open: who killed Marilyn Sheppard?

The Ballad
of Blind Love

Denise Labbé and Jacques Algarron (France)

A provincial philosopher, both cultivated and narcissistic. A woman, brave enough to raise a child on her own, hopelessly falls in love. Down a perverse spiral of trials testing her love, she now must do what for any woman would be unspeakable.

J acques Algarron was an eccentric young man. The twenty-four-year-old proclaimed himself to be a follower of Nietzsche, and in that corner of Brittany displaying one's philosophical knowledge had a dazzling effect on women: and his was at least as great as his innate elegance.

Denise Labbé was hungry for life and four years older than Algarron. She had been forced to work since she was very young, and yet she did not waste time feeling sorry for herself. On the contrary, she liked to enjoy herself and she liked men. Not even when she became pregnant by a young doctor who had no intention of recognizing his daughter did Denise lose her grit. Catherine was born in 1952, and Denise would sometimes leave her with her mother and sometimes with an affectionate wet nurse, Madame Laurent.

Soap and Water

Denise had never met anyone like Jacques. He spoke convincingly, and he explained to her that the purest bond between two people was based on total abnegation: true love, he said, can only be found in suffering and sacrifice.

Obviously, Jacques was not referring to his own love: he was careful not to sacrifice himself, while he forced the girl into every kind of physical and moral humiliation. Denise, blinded by the glamour of such a well-read boy, grateful for the privilege of receiving so much of his attention, accepted, complied with, and gave into a growing masochistic delirium that she mistook for loving devotion.

Algarron exploited her tendency to promiscuity, and drove her to seduce strangers in the street and bring them home. He delighted in watching their passion. Then, in a sadistic vicious circle, he expected Denise to ask him for forgiveness and punished her for giving herself to others. Jacques often humiliated her also in public view, beated her, he took pleasure in injure her back with a sharp pocket-knife, the same pocket-knife that she gifted him.

Perfect love requires the supreme sacrifice, Jacques would pontificate. And what sacrifice could be greater for a mother than killing her own child?

Jacques Algarron against the wall and Denise Labbé in tears after her arrest.

Your blood, your sacrifice will lead our love to be glorified forever and ever.

We are not sure whether Denise hesitated before sacrificing her little girl. The fact is that the plan failed three times.

The first time, Denise tried to throw Catherine off a balcony. The second time, she dropped her into a canal in Rennes during a walk, but the little girl was saved by a miracle. On October 16th, 1954, in Villelouvette, Denise pushed Catherine into the River Orge, but some passersby noticed the girl screaming in the water.

Relentlessly, on November 8th, 1954, Denise went to see her daughter in Vendôme, at the house of Madame Laurent, who had no suspicions about the little girl's repeated accidents. In the courtyard, Denise suggested that Catherine wash her rag doll in a wash tub. Denise picked up her daughter. Suddenly Denise flipped Catherine upside down, holding her by the ankles, and without hesitation plunged her head into the soapy water. The little girl flailed.

It takes several minutes to drown someone, even a child. However, this time – the fourth – Denise was determined to finish the job, and held Catherine firmly until she was sure that the girl had drowned. The little girl had only two years old.

Cross Fire

That very evening, Denise was arrested for the murder. Jacques abruptly dissociated himself from her, the murderous mother.

During the trial, both were subjected to psychiatric examination and declared fit to plead.

Without hesitation, they ruthlessly blamed each other. Denise accused the man of dominating her, of destroying her free will, of leading her sadistically to commit a crime that she would never have wanted to commit. Jacques denied doing or saying anything that could make Denise believe that he desired the child's death. Each could have exonerated the other by assuming responsibility for the crime. But neither did so.

They were both convicted: Denise got life in prison, and Jacques 20 years of forced labor for instigating the crime.

We are left with the mystery of the underlying reason for this terrible murder. Why did a woman like Denise, capable of seizing what life offered with both hands, kill her daughter? Was she a victim or an inhuman executioner?

LITERARY EVOCATIONS

The crime of the lovers from Vendôme, as the press immediately called it, has various literary evocations. Vendôme is the small town where Honoré de Balzac set *The Mysterious Mansion*, a noir story that is at once enigmatic and suspenseful.

The story of Denise and Jacques also seems to retrace in a disturbing way the plot of *L'innocente* by Gabriele D'Annunzio, of whom Algarron was a fervent admirer: the novel tells the story of a wealthy couple who leave to die, in the cold night air, a child the woman had in an extramarital relationship.

The writer Marcel Jouhandeau, who once said he's always had "a weakness for the guilty", followed every detail of the Labbé-Algarron trial and reflected on the enigmatic figure of Denise. There was in her, he argued, "something of Medea, who did not hesitate to kill her children, and does not grieve at their death but triumphs at it. When asked what she still has left she replied: *Myself. / I say myself, and that's enough.*"

Jean Cocteau, fascinated by the psychological complexity of the case, called it "the trial of the century".

We will never know just how subjugated Denise was by Jacques, or how lost she was in the narcissistic delirium that would completely crush her. We will never know whether Jacques explicitly, peremptorily asked for that sacrifice, or if he simply suggested it, in a game of cruel allusions that she was unable to win.

Neither will we ever know the extent to which Denise, blinded by a surprising egoism and by the illusion of being able to live a different life, launched herself beyond her lover's intentions.

Perhaps it was the image of her father dead in a pond (officially the man committed suicide, but it is more likely that he was drunk) that drove her toward a murderous act that – in symbolic repetition, in search of catharsis – might free her of her past. In any case, a plummet into the depths of the soul.

The Gentian Bitters Crime

Christel Müller and Wilhelm Leinauer (Germany)

Four young friends, two betrayals, a bottle of liqueur, and a death from poisoning. A shot of Gentian bitters kills the wrong person: this story of a flawed but fanciful crime shook all of Bavaria.

Distraught, Manfred buried his face in his hands. In the next room the doctors fought to save the life of his friend, Albert. It was his fault. If only he had been more careful. If only he had gotten rid of that bottle of Gentian bitters as soon as it had arrived as an anonymous gift! The more he thought about the package with its "Greetings from the Palatinate! Drink alone and with relish", the more clearly he realized that the real intention of the unknown sender had been to kill him! He could not imagine who could harbor such hatred for him. While absorbed in these thoughts, he felt a hand on his shoulder and, without protest, rose and followed a young policeman to the neighborhood precinct.

Do Opposites Attract?

Christel and Manfred Müller, married for three years, with two children, could not have been more different. Manfred was methodical and laborious, and dreamed of getting a permanent German government job one day: he had dedicated his life to this end, accepting postings that kept him far away from his family for weeks at a time. Christel, instead, loved in all things, including her sex life, fun and transgression. She hated being restricted by schedules, programs, or routines. Her enthusiasm and unrestrained vitality often exhausted Manfred.

The differences between them became ever more marked as time went by, until the beautiful Christel began to cast her eye around. The lucky person it fell upon was Wilhelm Leinauer, a curly-haired auto-mechanic the same age as Manfred, twenty-five. Wilhelm, too, was married, although the sweet and submissive Viktoria had very little in common with her fiery husband.

Unaware of the betrayal by their respective partners, Viktoria and Manfred continued to go out to parties and dinners as a foursome, and very soon malicious tongues began to wag in Kempten.

A Mysterious Package

On February 10th, 1967, Manfred, who was in Fürstenfeldbruck training for work in the national meteorological office, received an unexpected package. He did not recognize the address of the

---

On the left, Wilhelm Leinauer; on the right, Leinauer's lover and accomplice Christel Müller.

sender in Neustadt, but since he had attended a course there in the past, he thought that it might be from one of his old class-mates. The package contained a box of chocolates and a ceramic bottle of Gentian bitters, a liqueur found all over Germany.

On the advice of Albert Blumoser, his roommate at the time, Manfred put the bottle aside to await a suitable occasion to open it, and then went off to meet his wife. When he returned to Fürstenfeldbruck he found Albert with a bad cold. Something alcoholic was called for to alleviate the symptoms and Manfred remembered the anonymous gift. He poured out two glasses. Albert drank his off in one swallow and said: "This stuff tastes like vinegar!"

Alarmed, Manfred rushed to the bathroom and spit out the liqueur he had begun to drink. On his return he saw that Albert was in a bad way: his face was pale, his lips were blue and he couldn't breathe. They went to the hospital immediately, but there was nothing they could do for Albert. Two hours later he was dead. The autopsy revealed the cause of death: poisoning by ingestion of hydrogen cyanide (also known as prussic acid) contained in the bottle of Gentian bitters.

Weasels, Poison, and Love Tests

At first, suspicion fell on Gerd Fischer, Christel's former hus-band and the father of her first child. But this line of inquiry led nowhere, and the investigation very soon became bogged down. Things began to move again only when a friend of Wilhelm's, Konrad Reisacker, who owned a galvanizing and metal treat-ment plant, contacted the police. Konrad claimed that Wilhelm Leinauer had asked him for some prussic acid some days before the homicide. According to Konrad, Wilhelm had said that he needed the prussic acid to get rid of a weasel that was killing chickens at the country house he'd inherited from his father. Wilhelm was questioned and confessed, telling the police where he had hidden the rest of the poison on the farm, from where it was duly recovered. The revelation of his affair with Christel then led to her arrest, and she admitted her guilt.

The trial was held in Munich in an orgy of media coverage, such was the public interest in this lethal cocktail of sex, betrayal and poison. Under interrogation, Wilhelm and Christel gave two different motives for committing the crime. According to Wilhelm, the poison was only supposed to cause a mild stomach upset and a little diarrhea to the unfortunate husband, which would have allowed the wife to get away for a free weekend with her lover. For Christel, instead, the package was to be a kind of "love test": if Manfred kept quiet about the mysterious gift, this would have confirmed her suspicion that her husband had an adulterous relationship with a woman in Neustadt.

Both the accused were condemned to 15 years in prison for attempted homicide and culpable homicide. Manfred and Viktoria, in spite of everything, continued to believe in the good faith of their respective partners.

The Vitriol Mystery

Claire and Youssef Bebawi (Italy)

A pistol, a vial of vitriol, and a knot impossible to undo. This trial, which from 1964 until 1968 held Italy with bated breath, tarnished with blood and horror the "dolce vita" of Rome.

Taking a deep breath of the morning breeze, people cooled their emotions after the follies and excesses of the weekend. On Monday the city was slowly coming around: children sulkily put on their smocks, picked up their school bags and took to the streets; besuited bankers and lawyers walked deep in thought, thinking of their days crowded with commitments; housewives lost themselves in the colorful bustle of the market . . .

Also Karin Arbib, a secretary in the textile firm Tricotex, was hurrying to the office. She went up to the third floor of Via Lazio 9, opened the door, and was met by an inexplicable silence.

Suddenly the telephone required her attention. They were asking for news of her boss, Farouk Chourbagi, a twenty-seven-year-old Egyptian millionaire, the son of the ex-Minister of the Treasury. His fiancée, Countess Patrizia de Blanck, had waited for him in vain Saturday evening, to go to a party, and had still not been able to contact him. Karin was worried: she went to Farouk's office. It was an appalling sight. There was a corpse on the floor, in a pool of blood, its face unrecognizably disfigured by vitriol.

The body was identified by means of documents: it was none other than Farouk Chourbagi. The autopsy placed the hour of death between 5.45 and 6.15 on the evening of Saturday, January 18th.

A Suspicious Journey

The investigation began immediately, and the police were immediately put on the right track by Karin herself. Her boss had everything a young man might desire: a Mercedes and a Rolls-Royce in the garage, glamour, a high-class family . . . Quite enough to attract admirers and lovers.

But only one woman had been able to capture Farouk's heart and mind: Claire Ghobrial Bebawi, the wife of Youssef Bebawi.

This is the testimony of one of the most profound love stories ever told. It is something I've been so deeply involved in that it's changed my very nature, my entire being [...] I made the mistake at the beginning of abandoning myself to someone incapable of feeling emotion, a person unable to love. [...] However I'm in love with you and I'm sure I'd be devastated if you left me. (Farouk to Claire)

The charming Claire Ghobrial Bebawi and her husband, Youssef Bebawi, both in charge with the murder of the woman's ex-lover, the Egyptian millionaire Farouk Chourbagi.

The police found the woman and the husband at the Hotel Esperia in Athens. In a short time, the couple's movements were reconstructed. On Saturday they had made an incredible journey: Lausanne, Rome, Naples, Brindisi, Athens. In Rome, the Bebawis had stayed at the Hotel La Residenza, a stone's throw from the Farouks' apartment, precisely between 5.00 and 6.30 that evening, January 18th.

When the Lausanne police searched the Bebawi's apartment, they found two pistol holsters, one for a .38 caliber and one for a 7.65mm, the weapon that had fired four bullets into the head and back of the victim. Claire's face and hands were also covered in light burns, which could have been caused by vitriol. The woman stated that they were due to an accident at home, but there were too many coincidences not to arouse the investigators' suspicions. An arrest warrant was issued for the couple.

At first, Youssef and Claire declared that they were innocent. But when they arrived in Italy, perhaps by chance, perhaps strategically, their behavior changed radically. The couple confessed that they had gone to Rome, that they had "visited" Farouk and killed him, and that they had then headed for Naples. There, they said, they had gotten rid of the pistol and the vial of vitriol; they had then taken refuge in Athens. Their versions of the story, however, differed on a fundamental point: who had, in fact, killed Farouk?

Claire accused Youssef. Youssef accused Claire.

And the truth, apparently so near at hand, was quickly buried by an avalanche of lies and complaints.

Claire and Youssef Bebawi's marriage, which at the beginning was happy, began to crumble after the couple's move to Lausanne. Claire, who was used to being part of the jet set, to moving between fashionable parties, trips, and boutiques, felt imprisoned in her Swiss villa, which was ever more lonesome because of Youssef's frequent business trips. It was in that period that she met Farouk, who was immediately entranced by her. News of their relationship quickly spread in their circles. Youssef, who was a stranger to that world, at the beginning knew nothing, but he became suspicious of his wife's continuous absences. When he learned of the affair he furiously wrote to Farouk: "You're a filthy degenerate. My wife will no longer live in my home." And to Claire: "You can go. Don't wait to marry your lover boy." He went to Khartoum and converted from Orthodox Christianity to Islam to sign the repudiation of his wife. Farouk's parents, however, tried to prevent their son and Claire's marriage, since they were against the idea of their son marrying an older woman who'd been disowned by her husband. Claire continued to live in Youssef's home, but she commuted between Rome and Lausanne. Farouk began to see various other women, and became ever colder and more distant; she furiously accused him of ruining her life and abandoning her. Youssef, meanwhile, began a relationship with the German babysitter of his children, Gisela Henke, though he continued to be close to the Claire, who in any case was still the mother of his children.

The couple parted ways at the end of the trial. Youssef married Gisela Henke. Claire tried her luck as a tourist guide on the Nile.

It Was Him! No, it Was Her!

On May 21st, 1965, a courtroom in Rome prepared to host a trial that would make history. Public opinion was drawn to the famous attorneys involved in the defense of those described by journalists as a "diabolical couple". Giovanni Leone, the future President of the Republic, and Giuliano Vassalli, who was to head the Ministry of Justice and the Constitutional Court, and many other eminent jurists were present and ready for the battle of exhortations and rhetorical finesse. At 9.30 AM, the journalists were in the courtroom, notebooks in hand, prepared to write reams and reams, already describing the "Circe with green eyes" and her "Arab Othello". The *Corriere della Sera*:

> *Two mahogany doors, at the sides of the praetorium, opened almost at the same time: from the first came Youssef, without handcuffs, in a gray coat, white shirt, and crew-neck sweater. A fearful, timid, submissive, numbed, almost frightened face. From the second entrance came Claire: a star's entrance, wrapped in a Persian blond fur and mink stole, her dark blond hair combed with great care, her pale face without make-up and with a thin layer of powder. Two great, green eyes. Long gloves of finely worked leather, holding a white handkerchief.*

The sensuality with which the beautiful Egyptian woman crossed her legs, revealing a garter, sent the male audience into ecstasy; later, however, it took the side of the spouse whose honor had been offended. The female audience, on the other hand, waited in trepidation to know the details of the complicated love story between the "Egyptian tigress" and Farouk.

Alors elle a dit: I shot him, I shot him!

During the trial, the courtroom was transformed into a Babel of tongues: English, French, Italian, German, Arabic, Greek . . . The languages fought, intertwined, became confused, increased the confusion of an audience following the evolution of the trial with a morbid, almost excessive, interest.

Youssef stated that he had gone as far as Farouk's office with

Claire, who intended to finish the relationship with her lover, that he had waited at the main door, and that she had confessed to the murder to him. Claire, for her part, admitted that she had gone to Farouk's office, but that Youssef had arrived shortly afterward, and had started to argue fiercely with Farouk; terrified, she had hid in the bathroom, and from there she heard the gun shots.

Over time there was crying, testimony, conflict, exhortations. There were various *coup de théâtre*: first, one of the jurors was disqualified, thus leading to an annulment of the trial. Then Leone withdrew from Claire's defense.

After one year, 130 sittings, and jury deliberations of 29 hours, the verdict was reached: Claire and Youssef Bebawi were acquitted for lack of evidence.

The juridical principle *in dubio pro reo* prevailed, recalled by the defense:

> *The problem is not to understand who had the most obvious motive to kill: you must be certain of who killed. If you are not certain, you must acquit both the accused, because justice and civilization demand this. It is not uncivilized to acquit the person who committed a crime; but it would be uncivilized to convict an innocent person.*

Years afterward, an appeal court overturned the verdict. But it was too late. The accused were long gone: she had returned to Egypt, and he to Switzerland, and in neither of these countries was there an extradition agreement with Italy. In any case, the sentence was: 22 years for him, and 24 years for her; it was then confirmed by the Italian Supreme Court.

The Secret Life of a Voyeur

Camillo Casati Stampa (Italy)

Sex, money, blood and torrid deprivation: these were the ingredients of the crime in Via Puccini committed by the last heir to one of the most illustrious Italian aristocratic families, the Marquis of Soncino. Camillo Casati Stampa's victims were his wife Anna Fallarino and the woman's young lover, Massimo Minorenti. It was a scandal that resounded around Rome, with all the spicy trimmings to set the yellow presses rolling.

August 30th, 1970. 6.30 PM. Camillo Casati Stampa was in the attic of Via Puccini 9, a beautiful residence close to Villa Borghese and Via Veneto, in the heart of worldly Rome. He had rushed back from a hunting trip in Valdagno – he'd been unable to sleep, thinking it over – to go into what was going on between his wife and Massimo Minorenti. The Marquis called his butler and gave him simple but strict instructions: he was not to be disturbed by anyone. His voice was dry, his look dark and his face pale. He couldn't hide the inner suffering that troubled him. Dismissing his servant, he went into the drawing-room where Anna and Massimo were already awaiting him. He closed the door and locked it.

9.00 PM. The butler, together with Anna's sister, Velia, and Cesare Marangoni, a family friend, broke down the door of the drawing-room and stepped inside. The scene they found was horrifying: Anna was stretched out on a divan, her body torn to pieces by three gunshots; Massimo was found a little further

Camillo Casati Stampa, Marquis of Soncino, and the wife Anna Fallarino at theatre.

in, behind a small upturned table, shot in the head, his skull shattered. Camillo lay on the floor, his face disfigured by the final shot, his conclusion to the massacre. Five shots in all, the full magazine capacity of the 12-gauge Browning shotgun he'd used. The Marquis had evidently planned his movements well, calculating every action before entering the room. An hour later, the investigators arrived at the scene of the crime and began to piece together the elements of the tragedy.

"My Love, Love of my Life, Forgive Me"

The investigators quickly unearthed that most classic of motives, jealousy. But other, surprising elements soon emerged, leading the investigators to see the relationship between Camillo and Anna as something quite particular, and rather perverse. A diary with a green cover found in the Marquis' study explained everything. The numerous annotations gave precious testimony to ten long years of marriage, and made it obvious that the man was an authentic voyeur. He took pleasure in watching his wife have sex with others, while limiting himself to the amusement of watching close-up.

> *Anna drove me crazy with pleasure today. She made love with a soldier in such an effective way that even I could participate in the joy, but from far away. It cost me 30.000 lira, but it was well worth it.*

The Marquis' diary was full of similar extracts. It turned out that Anna had discovered this inclination of her husband on their honeymoon: she had decided to play along with him and became his accomplice, as was confirmed by more than 1500 photographs that were also found in the Marquis' study. In the pictures the woman was often naked or scantily dressed, in provocative poses and sometimes accompanied by a lot of men.

Generally they were perfect strangers from the less fortunate social classes, people the couple came across by pure chance in places where they could least expect to meet members of high society. Once identified, these men were approached and used by the Marquis to satisfy his personal pleasure.

In such a context, Massimo Minorenti was an exception to the rule. He was a young student of political science, getting bad grades, but good-looking and sure of himself. Massimo, who had the reputation of being a Don Juan, met Anna at a reception. The woman found him immediately attractive, and so involved Massimo in her erotic games with her husband. In the beginning Camillo saw nothing wrong in the affair: as far as he

THAT VILLA IN THE FOG

In the warm summer months, the Marquis and his wife left Rome to stay in an elegant residence in the heart of the Lombardy, on the edge of Arcore. The splendid mansion, encircled by a large park, is famous today as the Villa San Martino. As a result of the death of the Marquis and the wife, the villa was inherited by Camillo's daughter, Annamaria, who was at the time legally a minor.

The management of her wealth – and the debts owed by her father – was entrusted to her tutor, Cesar Previti, a lawyer. He persuaded Annamaria to sell the residence since a buyer had already come forward, an affable entrepreneur by the name of Silvio Berlusconi. Negotiations were concluded in 1974 for a sum of 500 million lira, considerably below the real value of the residence. But to Annamaria it mattered only that she could forget the past and turn her back on everything that was connected with her much talked about father, including that luxurious and elegant villa half hidden in the mists of Lombardy.

was concerned one lover was as good as the next, provided that they excited and amused his wife. But something unexpected happened: Anna fell seriously in love with Massimo, and the Marquis was profoundly upset. In his diary the last comments expressed fear about this unexpected development, and pain at having lost control of the situation. "The biggest disappointment of my life. I would prefer to be dead and buried. How awful!" he wrote in an obvious state of agitation.

Thoughts of suicide began to cross Camillo's mind. But then he decided to change plans, perhaps at the last moment, and take revenge on the two lovers as well. At the scene of the slaughter the investigators found a goodbye message written on the back of an erotic calendar:

My love, love of my life, forgive me, but I must do what I am about to do. Goodbye, my only last joy.

What to all appearances seems to be a sad note on which to leave, a last goodbye before the extreme gesture, was in fact the bitter verdict of a trial in which Camillo had played the triple role of prosecutor, judge and executioner.

Portrait of a Strange Couple

After such a tragedy, it was natural for the press and investigators to try to reconstruct the personality of the Marquis. A man of little culture, not very attractive and with reactionary ideas, Camillo Casati Stampa inherited a fortune but nothing of the intellectual stature of his illustrious forebears, among whom were Gabrio Casati, a senator of the nascent Regno d'Italia, and Alexander Casati, also active in politics and a minister many times over. Completely indifferent to the social and cultural changes that were taking taken place around him, Camillo had spent his life traveling, attending receptions and horse races, fighting boredom and hiding all his most intimate perversions.

What precisely in the figure of the Marquis had struck a beautiful and attractive woman like Anna Fallarino? On their first encounter, in the summer of 1958, they were both already married, but disillusioned and unhappy. Anna came from a modest family. As a child she had lived in poverty, and therefore she married the first man she met whose wealth might guarantee them a good social position. But by then, wealth wasn't enough for her. Perhaps in Camillo she saw a way to further up society's

A COMPLEX PSYCHOANALYTICAL PICTURE

The acclaimed psychoanalyst Professor Emilio Servadio, in the pages of the weekly magazine *L'Europeo*, was soon involved in the Casati Stampa Affair. After consulting the available documentation, Servadio drew a psychological portrait of the Marquis in which voyeurism was accompanied by other tendencies, masochism and probably latent homosexuality. According to the learned professor, the masochism of Camillo emerged in a desire to command and direct the sexual activity of his wife, and he did this by playing the role of organizer and director of the amorous episodes.

In this respect, when Camillo realized that he did not have any influence over the relationship between Anna and Massimo, he lost his position of power. According to Servadio, this loss triggered the homicidal reaction of the man. Moreover, the choice not to participate actively in the intercourse hid the identification of the man in the figure of the woman, and therefore suggested a latent homosexuality that the Marquis had tried to repress.

ladder, or maybe she was impressed by his noble behavior. They were married quickly, with the Marquis finding it child's play to have their previous marriages annulled by the Holy See, although he had a daughter, Annamaria, by his first wife.

In the course of the years their union appeared to work perfectly. Their friends considered them a serene and well-matched couple. Only the servants whispered about certain strange behavior by the Marquis. But it wasn't very important, not enough to arouse the interest of the press that was always looking for gossip about high society. It took the appearance of Massimo Minorenti to upset the equilibrium that had been established and that, in Camillo's mind, would probably have lasted for all eternity. Fate played a brutal card against the Marquis, and the glorious dynasty of the Casati Stampa ended its days on the pages of the Italy's most vulgar scandal magazines.

In the Name of Sappho

Marion Ihns and Judy Andersen (Germany)

The love between two women who bore in their souls the marks of male violence; the violent death of a wife-abusing greengrocer; and sentences that remain controversial: light punishment for the killer, life in prison for those who hired him. And in the background, the German feminist movement ready to fight, and a public thirsting for morbid details.

The life of Wolfgang Ihns, the owner of a grocery in Hamburg, had the infallible precision of a Swiss watch. After purchasing fresh fruit and vegetables early each morning, he worked without pause until lunchtime; he then took a refreshing nap in the basement of the store. Nothing had ever disturbed that routine since he and his wife Marion had started the business. That is, until October 20th, 1972.

A Professional Job

On the afternoon of that day Marion was suspicious of her husband's absence, which was longer than usual. She went down to look for him in the basement and found him lying in a pool of blood. She rushed for help, but when the doctors arrived they could only certify the man's death.

An investigation sprang into action, and one element immediately caught the attention of the police: the victim had first been hit with an ax handle and then stabbed in the heart. It was a brutal, cold-blooded murder, certainly the work of a professional killer. But who would want the greengrocer dead? Inves-

Marion Ihns, in charge with the murder of her husband Wolfgang.

tigators sifted through Wolfgang's life, looking for debts, vices, possible enemies, but in vain. At least in appearance, the man led an impeccable life. So they were left with Marion.

After the murder, she had moved to the house of a Danish friend, Judy Andersen. By intercepting telephone calls between the two women, the police discovered that Judy had contacted a man named Denny Pedersen (twenty-five), in Copenhagen. The young man was detained by the Danish police, and confessed that he had been paid by Marion and Judy to kill Wolfgang Ihns. It was they who had given him instructions for the murder, supplied the weapons, and let him into the basement so that he could wait for the arrival of his prey.

The fog surrounding the motive for the crime was dispersed by the discovery of the real nature of the relationship between Judy and Marion: for seven years the two women, besides chatting and sharing interests and dreams, had moved their friendship onto a much less platonic level, and had started an affair.

Difficult Lives

"It can't be true!" This exclamation had accompanied Marion all her life. It described the attitude she had always had toward events too great for her, events often cruel in their inevitability.

She was born in Hamburg in 1938, and soon had to deal with the death of her father, who went missing in Stalingrad, and the indifference of her mother, who only saw in the girl another mouth to feed. She was only nine years old, her beauty just beginning to bloom, when she suffered her first violence, being the victim of the brutality of a neighbor.

Her relationships with men were always unfortunate. First

engaged to a man named Heinz, she surprised him in bed with her sister; then there was Jürgen, a friend of her mother's, an alcoholic; finally, in 1965, she met Wolfgang. After the birth of their first daughter, Karen, her husband turned out to be hot-tempered and violent, and over the years he caused her to have several miscarriages. Marion's situation seemed to improve when she began an affair with a man named Peter, but that relationship was brusquely interrupted by the man's untimely death.

It was meeting Judy that gave Marion the happiness that she had desired for so long. Judy was ten years younger than she was, and she, too, had a difficult past behind her: she had suffered violence at four years old, had a stepfather who regularly beat her mother, and had endured an impoverished upbringing in the working-class district of Copenhagen.

An Unexpected Conviction

Although 1968 had stirred up emotions and given rise to deep changes in society, in the early 1970s homosexual relationships continued to be condemned. When news of the case spread, the

THE TRIAL AND THE FEMINIST MOVEMENT

The story of Marion and Judy became a symbol of the struggle for gay rights and equality in Germany. The German feminist movement organized strikes and protest demonstrations against what appeared to be clear discrimination against homosexuals and women in general. In that context, the well-known feminist journal EMMA was founded. It was financed and edited by Alice Schwarzer, the author of the famous book *The Little Difference and its Huge Consequences*. The journal is unique in that its editorial department has been composed, since 1977, only of women.

Federal Republic of Germany of Willy Brandt was scandalized and followed the trial, which took place in Itzehoe in 1974, with voyeuristic interest.

Every detail of the relationship between Judy and Marion was made public. The judges who authorized open sessions of the court did so assuming that prejudice against lesbianism would not influence the outcome of the trial. Nevertheless, the opinion became widespread that it was precisely the homosexual nature of the relationship that had "led them astray," and led them to plot the murder.

Marion was depicted by the newspapers as fragile and vulnerable, at the mercy of men who had humiliated her since childhood. Judy was given the dominant role, which was emphasized by the typically male job she performed: she was a crane operator. The court, however, was unable to establish which of the two women had first had the idea of killing Wolfgang. In the meantime Denny, the material perpetrator, was treated with generosity by the court and by public opinion for his willingness to collaborate. Tried by a Danish court, he was unexpectedly given only 16 years in prison. Marion and Judy, however, received life sentences.

One Death too Many, Admiral

Emilio Massera (Argentina)

There was one dead man too many in the ruthless criminal career of admiral Emilio Massera, Commander of the Argentinian Navy. He was the leader of the military coup that overthrew the government of Isabel Perón in 1976. He was responsible for the disappearance, torture or murder of tens of thousands. To this frightful amount let's add the homicide of Fernando Branca, husband of Massera's lover, Marta Rodríguez McCormack.

A most ambitious man, Emilio Massera often said:

It is my mother's fault that I have not become president of Argentina. In this country, after a military coup, only the head of the army can be number one. But my mother enrolled me as a boy in the Navy College.

General Jorge Rafael Videla, Commander of the Army, became president after the military coup of 1976. But everyone knew that the real leader was admiral Massera. He conquered the top position not only by his political ability but also by transforming the ESMA, the Navy mechanical school, into the greatest center of torture and murder in Argentina. Thousands of young men and women came to a horrible end there. Besides his political and repressive activities, Massera led a worldly life that fed the scandal pages. The admiral ("El Negro", as his friends called him) was married for years to Delia "Lily" Vieyra – an ugly woman who had the saving grace of having a rich father. Very soon, though, Messera begun to boast of relationships with starlets and opera singers. He was a handsome man, brilliant and brilliantined, with a great sly smile, and always ready to please. Power added further allure to his natural gifts.

The Other Daughter

Again, another mother's mistake: this time it was old Mrs. Mc Cormack, who practically offered her daughter Cristina (who she feared would become a spinster) to Massera. But the bold Emilio, on dropping by their place, fell in love with Cristina's much more attractive sister, Marta. The Rodríguez McCormack family belonged to Buenos Aires high society, and Marta, posed as a *grand dame*, was refined and poised. At a young age she was left widowed by César Blaquier, one of the wealthiest men in Argentina. Shortly after Blaquier's death, she was already engaged, and quickly married, to Fernando Branca, lately divorced from his first wife, Ana Maria Tocalli. Naturally, Marta's new husband was also very rich. He had been a warder in the Buenos Aires jail and rumor had it that he made his money by doing favors for

---

The admiral Massera, known as "El Negro", Commander of the Argentinian Navy.

certain prisoners. Then he had invested this money, acquiring land and real estate, and growing flax for linen and paper mills. It was only natural that the inheritance of the beautiful Marta should join that of Branca. It has never been clear whether the relationship between Massera and Marta started when she was still a single fiancée, or later, after she had remarried. But it is certain that for the admiral, Rodríguez McCormack was not an adventure like the others that filled up the newspapers – as with the explosive Graciela Alfano, for example.

The relation with Marta was absolutely different for him. He had really fallen in love

said a witness at the trial.

Love and business were mixed together very soon. Marta Rodríguez McCormack was worried because her husband, Fernando Branca, could not get credit from the Central Bank for $ 1.6 million that he had coming from the United States. The bank claimed that the money had dubious origins, perhaps deriving from illicit trafficking. But Fernando was concluding an important deal and he needed the money. Who better than admiral Massera to intervene, thought Marta, the woman of both men. All the more, the president of the Central Bank was rear admiral Andrés Covas, appointed to that important position by "El Negro" himself. Thus one day Branca was received by the admiral, who gave him a letter of introduction to Covas. "In two hours, the bank not only freed the money, but they immediately laundered it," Branca's son Fernando Junior explained: "And from that moment on my father liked Massera and began to do business with him."

The two shared the same woman, did deals together, and even planned to set up a bank. But Branca underrated the admiral, and tried to sell him land at a price much more than it was worth.

I Am the Clever One

The true problem for Fernando, perhaps, was his wife. It all fell apart during Holy Week in 1977, when the couple went to Punta del Este for a few days with two couples of friends. Maybe it was an attempt by Fernando to reconstruct his marriage with Marta, but on the third day a furious argument burst out between the two. The friends testified that Marta screamed at her husband, "You owe it all to me! Whatever you have, you've obtained thanks to me!" It was in that very moment that he signed his death sentence. He answered in front of everyone:

I am the clever one, stupid. It's me! I've screwed you all, including Massera. I've sold him junk and he didn't even notice.

The retort of the wife was tremendous. "I'm going to break this son of a bitch! When I get back to Buenos Aires I'm telling El Negro you wanna screw him, and he'll run you down with a truck!" By then the situation between the two had broken down and the following day, right in the middle of another public argument, Fernando slapped Marta twice.

That's enough! – she screamed furiously – *I'll tell Massera you've screwed him. And then God help you.*

Was it for money or jealousy? Shortly after the argument, Massera invited Branca to go boating. "He fell into the sea, I didn't see him again," the admiral would say on returning to port. The body of the betrayed husband would never be found, one more *desaparecido*, like the thousands who disappeared at the ESMA. But this was a murder that had nothing political about it. Long before justice could be rendered for all the other victims of "El Negro", on June 21st, 1983, the judge Oscar Mario Salvi had the admiral arrested for the homicide of Fernando Branca.

Too Many Loves for Delia

John Delia, Robyn Arnold and Robert Ferrara
(United States)

The corpse, wrapped in a discolored blanket, floated on the murky, gray Hudson River. Nothing surprising for New York in the late 1970s. The discoveries that followed, however, would shatter the suburb's image of middle-class calm. Behind row houses, manicured lawns, and smiling families an underworld lay hidden – of drugs, wild nights, and sex, in all its many forms.

John and Robyn. In spite of the gulf separating them, there was a strong understanding between them, so much so that John, who had always been openly gay, had left behind his previous inclinations for her, and seemed to want to get serious. They frequented the most fashionable clubs of the underground scene in Westchester County, just north of New York. John Delia was glamorous, a slight twenty-two-year-old with magnetic charisma. But he could also be vain and melodramatic: he loved to be the center of attention. The son of a building contractor, Delia had grown up in Riverdale, a residential district on the northern outskirts of New York.

As a child, he had often stayed at home with his mother, who would comb his hair and dress him up like a woman. He continued to like wearing women's clothes and, after studying art, began to perform in nightclubs in La Rochelle. And he did it as he liked it best: dressed in sequins and made up like the divas he admired. The gay clubs became his kingdom, and he began to accumulate conquests and lovers. He was good-looking, ironic, and shameless to the point that he'd wear nothing under his tight pants so that his tool could be intuited through the fabric. Perhaps it was only on the stage that he felt he could really be himself.

Neither was Robyn a normal girl: in that world of aspiring-to-be-something and hopeless young men she had an aura, like a princess of the suburbs. Robyn Arnold, her father's darling, grew up in private schools, tennis matches, and dance lessons. She was a surgeon's daughter, and had decided to become a nurse. Beautiful and self-confident, shameless but restless, she had found in that eccentric boy and his circle something that satisfied her desire to transgress, her need to escape the gilded cage in which she lived.

Robyn knew that John was not only gay, but that he had a confused sexuality: when she met him, he was following hormone therapy to begin the process of a sex change. This did not appear to disturb or discourage her. She was used to getting what she wanted, and this time she wanted him. John per-

---

A sketch showing a moment of the trial for the murder of John/Diane Delia; on the left the two defendants, Robert Ferrara and Robyn Arnold.

haps saw in her the chance for a "normal" life, the approval of his father and, something not to be taken lightly, a substantial amount of money in the bank. In fact, Robyn was John's most enthusiastic admirer, and she financially supported his career.

Change of Identity

When John announced the news of his engagement to Robyn, his father appeared astonished and relieved. The girl's parents reacted in a completely different way. Up to that point, they had thought their daughter's infatuation for John to be an amusement, a passing phase to be humored in order not to irritate her. But confronted with the prospect of marriage, their good humor vanished. In any case, it was not necessary to intervene: after meeting Robyn, John had stopped taking hormones. But then he had a change of heart and became determined, once again, to finish the interrupted process. He would have the operation and become a woman. Robyn was not even shocked this time: if it was what John wanted, he should have it. Her obsession with him was such that she said to herself:

If I can't have Delia as a lover, at least I can be his best friend.

It was she who paid the $ 5000 for the operation which, in November, 1980, transformed John into Diane, in honor of the singer Diana Ross. Diane moved to Canada and began to see men again, many men, even more than before, now driven by the desire to try out the new seductive power of her body. She spoke of her many conquests and disappointments with Robyn, as two friends would have done. Diane had in the meantime taken up with her old flame, Robert Ferrara. A boy with a troubled past, Ferrara grew up in a Pennsylvania town which was too small for his restlessness. He'd always shown his homosexual tendencies, which his parents disapproved of. He imagined he might find the chance he desired in the Navy, but very soon he fled from that too, committing the crime of desertion. He was given refuge by some friends outside of New York and began to work as a bar tender, becoming a minor figure in the wild nights Delia took part in. It was at the Playroom, a Club in Yonkers, that the two had met in 1978, when Diane was still John. They were both little more than twenty, gay and attractive, searching for a place in the world, with ambitions of breaking into fashion. There was an immediate attraction between them. They both had dark sides, however, which had led them both, several times, to attempt suicide.

I Declare You Husband and . . .

Perhaps in an extreme attempt to prove her femininity, Diane decided to conclude what she had been unable to finish with Robyn: she persuaded Robert to marry her. On August, 1981, having been recognized as a woman by the law, Diane became Mrs. Ferrara. Her wedding ring, three gold rings and diamonds intertwined, was a gift from the ever-present Robyn.

But Robert was gay. Diane's new appearance no longer attracted him, and he began to seek the satisfaction he couldn't find in the marriage bed. As for Diane, she lost little time in consoling herself with other men. There were months of rows and scenes, which often culminated in violent fights. In the end, Diane did what any other wife would have done: she left her husband and moved in with her trusted friend, Robyn. It was

October 4th, 1981. For a few days Diane and Robyn enjoyed themselves with other friends. Diane wanted to forget recent disappointments, and she was ready to do it at any cost. But she was too eccentric, and she wanted things centered on her, so tensions between the two girls increased. Now that they were playing on the same field, Robyn's wounded pride was awakened on the first occasion when they competed to conquer the attention of a young man. Robyn hit below the belt: "Mine is real", she said with a wink, referring to what Delia had obtained through surgery. But the worst was yet to come: Robyn, who wanted to be the only woman in Diane's life, saw her flirting with another woman. It really was too much. Robert, too, just like Robyn, was furious because Diane had left home and was going around clubs ready to throw herself on anyone, man or woman.

An Endless Night

On October 28th, 1981, police recovered a woman's body floating in the Hudson. She'd been killed some weeks before: four bullets in the head. There was something strange about the body. The doctors who examined it discovered that the person was transsexual. It then didn't take long to connect the missing girl, Diane, to the man who up to a year before had been called John Delia. But it was another three months before an arrest could be made. Investigators focused on the two most important people in Delia's life: both Robyn and Robert seemed to have reasons for killing Delia, but neither the weapon, nor any other proof were ever found. Only contradictions, lies, unresolved questions. Why had Robert pawned the engagement ring that Diane probably had on her finger at the time of death?

How did a girl like Robyn fit into that world? And what were the sandals doing in her cupboard, sandals that, according to witnesses, Diane was wearing the night she was killed?

Diane was seen for the last time on the evening of October 7th. She'd put on a lavender dress and high heels to go out with Robert, who had asked that they clarify the situation. He had a picked her up in Robyn's car, and then they had disappeared. It was easy to suspect that poor boy, a shady character, and gay, as well. The turning point came when the nurse Dominick Giorgio, Robert's new lover, was arrested for stealing synthetic cocaine from the hospital. In exchange for his freedom, Dominick betrayed his friends. Robert and Robyn were accused of premeditated murder.

A Trial for Two

According to Dominick's testimony, the accused had admitted, in his presence and in various situations, having committed the murder together. For this reason a single trial was organized. But this did not mean that all the evidence examined was necessarily valid against both.

Suddenly Robyn, who in the previous weeks had shared Robert's apartment and hung out with his friends, transformed into a haughty high-society girl, completely extraneous to that sordid world. She was already preparing to marry her new fiancé, a dentist, and denied her involvement with Delia:

I never loved him. It was only infatuation. No, not even that. It was the lifestyle. The excitement, the glamour. For a while, I found him interesting. Then I got tired of him. I'd had enough excitement.

Neither of the witnesses ever gave evidence: everything depended on the analysis of the possible motives and of the circumstantial evidence. Robyn had an alibi which protected her for the hours before the murder, but nothing excluded her from having joined Robert. In fact, the evidence pointed in this direction.

After more than a week, presumed new evidence came to light, a letter that Robert had written to none other than Dominick. It contained a confession, and it described the stages of the crime.

Robyn and Robert, after having obtained a weapon, had attracted the victim into the woods with an excuse:

Robyn shot her in the nape of the neck. I ran off. [Then I came back] and I fired twice at Delia, putting her out of her misery.

Robert did not deny writing the letter, which could be interpreted in several ways. The whole trial depended on the reliability of the key witness. Robert's attorney accused Dominick Giorgio of having produced false evidence to give greater credibility to his testimony, thanks to which he had been released. Could one trust a man who, to clear himself, had not hesitated in betraying the man who he'd said was his dearest friend? After Robert's imprisonment, Dominick had stayed in contact with him, writing to him and visiting him in prison, where he had tried to bring him drugs. Perhaps he had managed to obtain Robert's written confession by exploiting his dependence, or simply by taking advantage of Robert's faith in him, the only affection he still had in spite of everything.

Robyn's attorney, on the other hand, maintained that Dominick had acted in agreement with Robert. By delivering the let-

The figure of Robyn Arnold has many dark aspects. Some elements of her past which emerged during the trial were never clarified. When she was interrogated, she denied ever intending to marry John Delia, although Delia's parents and stepmother unanimously stated that the young couple were officially engaged. Some relations and acquaintances maintained that her real name was Roberta and that she had changed it, but Robyn determinedly denied these assertions. She had also stated that she had obtained a diploma from Syracuse University, but the only record found in the university register was for a Roberta Arnold, who attended for only one semester. Finally, Robyn stated that she was a professional nurse, and that she practiced as one, yet in the register of nurses qualified in New York State her name, either as Robyn or as Roberta, did not appear.

ter he had tried to cast guilt on his client, by making her appear as the main instigator of the murder, in the hope of reducing the seriousness of his lover's charge. In this way he was seen as a minor actor, almost as a merciful helper. He was able to exploit in this grey zone cleverly, suggesting to the jury:

You wouldn't dare to put your lives [...] in the hands of Dominick Giorgio. So don't put Robyn Arnold's life there either!

His words hit the mark. While Robyn was celebrating victory, Robert alone was found guilty and sentenced to a minimum of 20 years in prison. He was released in 2008.

A Well-respected Woman

Simone Weber (France)

With her good-natured face and the reassuring air of an ordinary middle-aged woman, Simone Weber could have played the grandmother in a fairy tale. Instead, she was nick-named the "Devil of Nancy". It is hard to imagine that the little old lady in the white blouse could have murdered and dismembered her former lover, who had decided he didn't want to see her anymore. Not even the efforts of twenty-five lawyers could argue away the damning evidence of her involvement in the disappearance of Bernard Hettier.

S imone Weber did not have an easy life. She was born in Loraine in 1929; her parents separated when she was hardly four years old, and their four children were divided between them. Little Simone, along with her sister Madeleine, to whom she was very attached, was entrusted to the father.

After an unfortunate marriage to an alcoholic husband, the woman found herself once again on her own, with five children to raise. She coped as best she could, resorting at times to less than lawful activity. But the death of two of her children within a short time, one from a drug overdose, the other committing suicide while in the military, affected her deeply and she began to suffer from a persecution complex.

The Seducer

She met Bernard Hettier in 1982. He was an interesting fifty-year-old divorcee from Maxéville. After some time their different perspectives on the relationship became clear. Simone became more possessive and suffocating from day to day. She expected exclusive attention from Bernard, and the man did not seem inclined to give this to her. So he tried to break off the relationship. The decision did not have the hoped-for effect. Indeed, the woman became increasingly nagging: in the following three years she pestered him with telephone calls, she stalked him, threatened him.

Then on June 22nd, 1985, after a violent argument with Simone, Bernard disappeared. That evening Monique Nus, the man's new lover, received a strange telephone call: the caller said that the man would not be going away with her for the weekend. Suspicious, and since Bernard had told her that Simone had threatened him, Monique sent her son to question the jealous former girlfriend. The son did not find Simone, but noticed Bernard's Renault parked in front of the woman's house, in Nancy. The following day the car was gone.

Simone Weber's impassive aplomb after the arrest.

Winning Numbers

Some days later, the family unexpectedly received news from Bernard's office that the man had asked to be excused from work on medical grounds. What looked like a hopeful sign of life turned out to be the first of a series of clues pointing to Simone: it emerged that the man examined by the doctor for the medical certificate was not in fact Hettier, but a young person who was actually the son-in-law of the main suspect.

The Haags, downstairs neighbors of Simone, revealed that on the night of June 22nd they had heard a thud coming from her flat, and then the sound of an electrical motor which was on for a long time. When they looked out through the spy-hole in the door, they saw the woman going up and down the stairs dragging large garbage bags towards her car.

Put under surveillance, Simone appeared to be a bizarre and eccentric woman. She seemed to call the shots, making the policemen follow her around, as if she was controlling them.

Her phone calls, apparently innocent, were mainly to her sister Madeleine who lived in Cannes; but when, giving her sister the "numbers of the lottery", she exceeded 49 (the highest one in the French lottery), the agents realized that the women communicated in code. The numbers were those of a telephone booth from which, in the dead of night, Simone contacted Madeleine. The conversation focused on a certain Bernadette, that is . . . the car of Bernard Hettier.

The discovery of the Renault in a garage in Cannes was the clue that the police were waiting for. The two sisters, under separate interrogation, didn't make concessions. They claimed that Hettier would have entrusted the car to Madeleine while he was away.

Simone's flat was searched and, besides a .22 rifle and a spent cartridge, they recovered an electrical circular saw with rental contract dated June 21st. The dots seemed to be lining up by themselves, giving a chilling picture.

Queen of the Courtroom

Simone Weber was arrested, but Hettier was still missing. All unidentified corpses found in recent months were checked again. Attention was concentrated on a male torso recovered from the river at Poincy en Seine-et-Marne on September 15th, 190 miles from Nancy but suspiciously near where Simone's daughter lived. The remains of the man, who was estimated to be about forty years old from the autopsy, were insufficient for making an unequivocal identification, but were declared to be compatible with those of Bernard.

A MYSTERY IN THE PAST OF SIMONE

The search of Simone's flat revealed instruments for counterfeiting documents and many papers, among which was a marriage certificate. It turned out that, in 1980, Simone had married an eighty-year-old man named Marcel Fixard. They had met through a dating service. A month after the wedding, the man died suddenly. Simone inherited his assets and pension. Only as a result of the investigation into the disappearance of Hettier was new light cast on that episode. It not only turned out that the testament in her favor was false, but also that the wedding had been contracted by someone recruited to impersonate Marcel Fixard. Moreover, it was discovered that eight days before the death of her husband, Simone had bought a drug for the heart that, administered in massive doses, could be lethal. At a distance of years, the homicide suspicion could not be proven and the case was archived.

The trial began on January 17th, 1991, after the accused had already spent more than five years in custody, pending trial. The trial lasted six weeks. In front of dozens of journalists and an enthralled audience, Simone's charisma prevailed. The woman, from behind a barricade of bourgeois respectability, alternated appeals to morality with words of deprecation towards acquaintances and witnesses. One after another she dispensed with the services of lawyers whose methods or strategy she did not approve of, including the celebrated Jacques Vergès. After expert's report had been given by a psychologist, Simone asserted:

> *Psycology is a not something in which I believe. From the beginning Dr. Scherer seemed not what I would call unpleasant, but a hundred times worse. On what formula is this judgment based? For him, I am only material to analyse . . .*

In spite of the absence of a confession and of irrefutable evidence, Simone Weber was condemned to 20 years jail for unpremeditated homicide.

In 1999 the woman was released. With her blue eyes wide open, she continues to proclaim her innocence.

The Mantis of Val Bormida

Gigliola Guerinoni (Italy)

Attractive, blue-eyed, with a penetrating gaze. Two failed marriages behind her, three children from different men, a long list of lovers. For ten years, Italian newspapers and magazines spoke only of her, Gigliola Guerinoni. They called her many things: Messalina, man-eater, bewitching, Circe... Mantis, like the insect whose female devours the male after mating. Murderess. But nobody ever understood who she really was.

On August 19th, 1987, on an escarpment of Mount Ciuto, inland from Savona, a technician for the local telephone company found the body of a man. The corpse was huddled up grotesquely and in an advanced stage of decay. It had been there for days, exposed to the heat and to animals. Someone had stove in his skull, made his face unrecognizable by beating it to a pulp, and then dumped him down the drop.

Identification was only possible due to a key ring engraved with the emblem of the pharmacists' association. This was found by the Carabinieri in the remains of the camp where the murderer had burned the victim's clothes.

This victim was Cesare Brin (fifty-six), a wealthy pharmacist from Cairo Montenotte, a municipality in Val Bormida. He was very well-known in the area for having been a councilman in the municipality, and also the president of the Cairo football club. It was said that he had frittered away most of his substantial family fortune to take team to the Series C, or third division league. While he once was known as "the Emperor", nobody had called him this for some time: the team had stopped winning and he'd fallen into debt.

In Cairo there was a person as famous as he was: his most recent lover, Gigliola, a forty-two-year-old gallery owner who had never bothered trying to hide her wild life.

Femme Fatale

Gigliola Guerinoni was born in Cairo on February 23rd, 1945. She studied to be a nurse, and married Andrea Barillari when she was only nineteen years old. She had two children with Barillari, and then they divorced: the role of wife and mother was not enough for her, and she felt a sense of repulsion for common people. She longed for something else. Something more.

In order to get on, she used the only means at her disposal: her beauty. It was men, who fell at her feet, who began to nourish her continual hunger for recognition.

After several relationships, Gigliola met Ettore Geri, an accountant well known for his extreme right-wing sympathies. He was twenty-seven years older than she was. For Gigliola, Geri left his job and his family, and invested his severance pay in the gallery that Gigliola had always dreamed of opening in Cairo. It was thus that they moved into the first floor in Via dei Portici. They were accomplices and would long remain so. This was taken to the extreme.

But Geri was soon forced to accept the fact that the woman could not be curbed. Thanks to him, Gigliola had finally obtained social recognition. And yet, when their daughter Soraya was born, her rebellious instinct was reawakened. She was persecuted by the specter of family life. Thus she officially brought Pino Gustini into her life. He was a painter who visited the gallery, and his move to Gigiola's home, with Geri and their daughter, created a scandal all over town. But ten years went by, and the ménage à trois was accepted in some way, and criticisms died down.

Late in 1986, Gustini died at the age of fifty-two. He'd suffered from a grave form of diabetes. Only then was it discovered that Gigliola had secretly married Gustini, while everyone took it for granted that she was Geri's wife.

The delicate equilibrium that the woman had constructed was collapsing. She reacted by starting yet another affair, this time with "the Emperor" of Cairo Montenotte.

Five Lovers for a Crime

With Cesare Brin she seemed assured of new economic and social advantages. He gave her presents, he showered her with flowers, he took her out to dinner, he even paid the rent for the gallery. However, problems very soon emerged. Gigliola realized that she was involved with a ruined man, a man heavily in debt. Thus she was brutally awakened from the greedy dreams she had entertained. Moreover, Brin was jealous and possessive, and she had always considered herself to be a free woman; she was proud and decisive, and had never had a passive role in life. She could not tolerate it.

On the evening of August 12th, some passersby heard strange noises coming from the apartment. Glass breaking and cries:

- I'll kill you!
- Be quiet, or they'll hear us.

Hours later, Gigliola's car came out of the garage. She was driving, and next to her was the body of Cesare Brin. There were also some of the woman's "admirers", called on to lend a hand. They drove as far Mount Ciuto and dumped the body.

On August 31st, 1987, Gigliola Guerinoni was arrested. Splattered blood had been found on the walls of her apartment, as well as pieces of skull and brain matter on the staircase. They also arrested Ettore Geri, for being an accessory. The quartet made up of the painter, Giuseppe Gardena, the deputy police commissioner Raffaele Sacco, the regional councilman Gabriele di Nardo, and Mario Ciccarelli, Brin's assistant, were also taken in. All of them were accused of obstruction of justice for attempting to conceal the corpse.

But what really happened at Via dei Portici?

A Thousand Truths for one Trial

Gigliola testified that on the evening of August 12th, two shady individuals had turned up at the house and spoken to Brin privately, demanding that a drug debt be paid. The argument had escalated and the two men had knocked Brin unconscious and taken him away. She had had no further news of him.

Ettore Geri's version was very different. He said that he had received a telephone call in which Gigliola told him that she did not feel well. She asked him to bring her a painkiller. When he arrived at Via dei Portici, he found Brin in the same bed that had been his for many years and, overcome by jealousy, Geri hit Brin with a bottle. In court he retracted, and maintained that he was innocent.

But there was another person present in the apartment at the time of the murder: Gigliola's daughter, Soraya, who had accompanied her father. When she was interrogated, she declared that her parents had wanted to eliminate Brin for some time and that in the phone call, the sentence "I have a headache" was actually the signal agreed to put the plan into action. At first she had stayed in the garage. But then, hearing noises inside, she feared for the life of her father, so she went up to the apartment with a hammer. That is when she saw Brin lying on the bed, his skull stove in.

Drop dead, bastard

Gigliola had hissed.

Geri maintained that these were only a young girl's fantasies, and Gigliola suggested that the confession had not been spontaneous. In any case, Soraya would later refuse to testify.

Guilty, Guilty, Guilty

During the trial, doubts arose over the death of Gigliola's second husband, Gustini: she was accused, with Geri, and of having provoked the man's death by not giving him the drugs he

KARMA STRIKES BACK?

On September 10th, 2013, two men set their mastiff on the policemen who had intervened in a brawl in a pizzeria in San Basilio, Rome. For some strange reason, they lost control of the dog which, instead of throwing itself on the police, attacked an old lady passing by. This was Gigliola Guerinoni, who was going back to the prison: for the first time, she was in the newspapers as a victim and not as a brutal murderer. She was bitten on the thigh, on the calf, on the buttocks, and on the hand, and was seen in the hospital emergency room. She had to undergo an operation. The animal was tied to a fence with a cord around its neck. It died of suffocation a few hours later.

needed for diabetes, and for delaying his admission to the hospital. Both were acquitted.

On the other hand, no one had any doubts about the Mantis' guilt in Brin's murder. She was convicted in the first trial, again in appeal courts, with the sentence being confirmed in the Cassation Court. She got 26 years in prison, 4 of which were for the defamation of the judge Maurizio Picozzi: she had stated several times that she had had an affair with him. She said that he was taking revenge on her for having left him. Geri was first acquitted and then sentenced to 15 years for being an accessory. Sacco, Ciccarelli, and Gardena were sentenced to 3 years in prison for concealment of the corpse. Di Nardo was acquitted on all counts.

She did not Change

Gigliola Guerinoni served the sentence in the prisons of Imperia, Venice, Opera, and Rome. During her sentence she continued to be the subject of gossip journalism, receiving letters from admirers and even proposals of marriage. In 1994 she married Luigi Sacripanti, another prisoner. It was her third marriage. They divorced four years later. In 2002 she obtained a work release: she only went back to Rebibbia jail in the evening, while during the day she ironed clothes in a vacation home run by nuns, near Piazza Navona. In March, 2014, the Court of Rome declared her sentence served.

The star attraction in the trial, she was flattered by the attention given to her. In her memoirs, and in numerous interviews, Gigliola has always maintained that she was innocent.

Assassin ! Assassin !

Carlos Monzón (Argentine)

Après une enfance misérable et le succès rencontré dans le monde de la boxe, Carlos Monzón était devenu un acteur renommé et une personnalité du jet-set international : la débauche, l'argent et les femmes apportaient une sorte de rédemption et de récompense pour les souffrances endurées dans sa jeunesse. Puis, tout à coup, il se réveilla brusquement de ce rêve et tout s'écroula autour de lui.

L e matin du 14 février 1988, l'actrice uruguayenne Alicia Muñiz mourut dans le jardin de la petite villa dans laquelle elle vivait à Mar del Plata, sur la côte atlantique, à quelques kilomètres de Buenos Aires. Ce fut, ce jour-là, la première nouvelle sur toutes les radios et les télévisions argentines : la défunte était en effet l'ex-femme du boxeur Carlos Monzón, dont elle était séparée depuis peu. Tous deux, le soir précédent, s'étaient rendus en compagnie de leurs amis d'abord au casino puis dans

heated quarrel, the woman had fallen from the first floor balcony: a thud, and then her lifeless body lay in a pool of blood on the ground. It was six o'clock, Valentine's Day, when lovers are celebrating all over the world. Desperate cries – it was Monzón – echoed all around:

Alicia threw herself from the balcony! Call an ambulance!

A Difficult Childhood, and then Boxing

Carlos Monzón was born on August 7th, 1942, in San Javier, Santa Fe Province. At the age of eight, he left school to help his parents maintain the family. He worked – and got by – in any way possible: he delivered mineral water, fresh milk, or the morning newspapers. He scraped together a little money by organizing wrestling matches with other boys in the district. He became a professional boxer and rapidly rose up the international rankings. In 1970 he gained the right to challenge the world middleweight champion, the Italian Nino Benvenuti. On November 7th, 1970, in the packed Palazzetto dello Sport in Rome, this almost unknown Argentinian, against all forecasts, knocked out his opponent, who was exhausted by Monzón's incessant punches. He would defend the title as many as 14 times before retiring unbeaten 7 years later (in a rematch, he took care of Benvenuti in only three rounds). He had an incredible right and a left jab that gradually demolished his opponents in the ring. He also had a considerable reach (he was more than 5 foot 11); and he was exceptionally able to take a punishment. Very few managed to defeat him. The last time he lost a fight was in 1964, early in his career.

Carlos Monzón, sentenced to 11 years in prison for the murder of his ex-wife Alicia Muñiz.

Success and Luxury

Carlos Monzón, wildly popular in Argentina, was also an acclaimed actor. On the set, he met and fell in love with the actress Susana Giménez. For her, he left his wife, María Beatriz, who he married when he was twenty. The story with Alicia began only after he hung up his gloves: it was his second marriage, this time with a child. He had a luxurious lifestyle, as if is to compensate for his previous poverty: champagne (only the best brands), a Rolex always on his wrist, shiny new sports cars to show off with pride, and before going out, floods of cologne, always Dior. His friends included the French actors Alain Delon and Jean-Paul Belmondo, and the stylist Pierre Cardin. He only wore designer clothes and was considered one of the most elegant men in the world. The tabloids related details and published photos of his love affairs with the most popular stars of the time, among whom was the icon of beauty and style, an undisputed sex symbol, Ursula Andress, the first Bond girl. Until that tragic morning came.

The Trial and the Sentence

Monzón was tried, found guilty, and sentenced to 11 years in prison. According to the scientific evidence, he had thrown Alicia off the balcony, causing various fatal fractures to the head. Then, confused or perhaps in contrition, he himself had jumped:

I jumped to save her.

He tried to justify this claim by showing his bandaged left arm, which had softened his fall. But as luck would have it, there was an eyewitness, a homeless man by the name of Rafael Crisanto Báez, who on that Sunday morning, as always, had set off with his cart in search of anything to sell, cardboard or glass bottles. From his toothless mouth came serious accusations against Monzón. He was close to house when the Monzón and Muñiz arrived in a taxi. He saw the light in the bedroom go on, heard Alicia call her ex-husband "jealous and neurotic", he saw Monzón, his self-control gone, put his hands around the woman's neck and lift her from the floor until she became unconscious: that body that moved desperately and at a certain point slumped, held in a lethal grip. Then – continued Báez – Monzón threw Alicia over the parapet of the balcony.

The results of the autopsy confirmed this: when the woman fell, she was unconscious or even dead. In a room a few meters away, their son was sleeping, unaware of everything.

It certainly was not the first time that Monzón had committed violence against a woman: all of his relationships had been accompanied by violence. His first wife, on being abused time after time, had finally shot her husband with a pistol (the bullet was still lodged in his shoulder). Alicia, tired of all this, had reported him several times. But then she obtained a separation.

A Sad Epilogue

When he was driven to the prison, with that ignominious accusation, stones and insults hit the black and white van. Inside a policeman patiently looked after him.

Murderer! Murderer!

shouted scores of women, ignoring the cordon of police escorting the procession of motor vehicles. He watched them, helpless, with lackluster eyes, his gelled hair combed back, as was his usual style. "Femicide", we would say today. On one of the busiest boulevards of Buenos Aires, there appeared a banner which read:

Let violence against women go unpunished no more.

He, who so many times had been praised and acclaimed by the crowd, now had to face the worst of defeats. He, who had almost never needed the verdict of the judges to be the winner, since he knocked out his opponents well within the end of the match, this time had to submit to the verdict of the judge, who, moreover, was a woman. This judge, on July 3rd, 1989, read the sentence, pronouncing every word distinctly. What awaited him was a cell three meters by four, with only a bed, a table, and a toilet. After a few years, he was granted semi-liberty.

On January 8th, 1995, Monzón returned to prison, his gray Renault 19 swerved and violently hit the guardrail on Provincial Road No. 1. The impact at high speed, nearly 90 miles an hour, hurled him from the car. A farmer, who quickly ran up after hearing the crash, found his lacerated lifeless body 160 foots from the car, which was reduced to wrecks. In this way the tale of the accursed champion ended. No opponent had ever put him on the canvas, but he was incapable of maintaining the lucidity he knew in boxing outside the ring, where, always waiting for him, was that life he had fought against with determination and pride since he was a boy.

The Black Widow

Linda Calvey (United Kingdom)

She began to play the role of gangster's moll when she was very young: she wasn't quite twenty when she met her Micky, on a Saturday evening. Micky was dead before she went with another. Since then she had seduced one criminal after another, making each her own. Nobody would ever have thought that the platinum blond with the innocent air could be so dangerous.

The British newspapers called Linda Calvey the "Black Widow", comparing her to the small black spider that eats her male partner after mating. A small red spot on the creature's abdomen warns of the poison contained inside. Nothing in Linda's appearance put the men who looked into her velvet eyes on guard.

Born on April 8th, 1948, in Ilford, a neighborhood of Greater London, at sixteen she had already had an affair with a married man; after four years of the relationship he still addressed her as "my little secret". But she was overflowing with vitality and expected her man to leave his boring wife. One Friday afternoon she said that she did not want to see him for a weekend, and that she needed to think over their affair.

She looked in the display window of the shop at the end of the road. There was an eccentric bright pink dress that would suit her. It would lift her spirits. Returning home, she met her cousin Patsy with her husband George, who completed the job of cheering her up. They invited her to a party for a friend of George's. The fellow had gotten out of jail recently and wanted to meet up with all his old mates. Linda had just bought her pink dress. She accepted the invitation. Though she wasn't sure she wanted to be pretty and sociable for a jailbird, a guy who probably had a broken nose and who wasn't very bright, she let herself be persuaded.

That evening at the bar, the two hit it off immediately. She forgot her married man and George's friend began to court her. A few months later they were living together in an old garage in the north-east of London. Micky was always involved in something. He managed to scrape enough money together from one hold-up or another. They lived for each other and took life as it came.

December 9th, 1978

Everything changed one afternoon, outside a supermarket in Eltham, on the south-eastern edge of London, when Micky attempted to steal £ 10.000 from a security van. It was a job he had scouted many times but had never got round to doing. Now he needed to get his hands on some money to buy Christ-

---

Linda Calvey's arrival to the Old Bailey, the criminal court of London.

mas presents for his wife and two kids, Melanie (eight) and Neil (four). On his way out he said to Linda: "See you for supper." But he would never return. Detective Michael Banks dropped him stone dead on the street, two slugs in the abdomen.

Linda was one of the last to learn of Micky's death. She had left the house to search for him and so missed the phone calls until the following morning.

On her own, she began a legal battle against the police because she claimed that her man had been shot in the back, and so killed unnecessarily by Banks.

It was at Micky's funeral that she met Ronnie Cook again. He was one of the accomplices in the ill-fated attempted robbery. Linda accepted that she would have to remake her life, now that Micky was no longer around. Ronnie was married and had three children, but that didn't stop him from being drawn into the Black Widow's web. He couldn't leave her alone. He loaded her with expensive gifts, showed attentions upon her, but also subjected her to threats in fits of jealousy. When he returned to jail in 1981, he asked his friend Brian Thorogood to look after Linda in his absence. Brian, needless to say, took him at his word.

Brian had 20 holdups under his belt, 16 of them armed: optimum qualifications to become Linda's new lover. She set to work with determination. By any measure, she became a full member of the gang, first as a lookout, then as a getaway driver, always ready to step on the gas as soon as they came running out with the loot.

In 1985, after the umpteenth robbery, they both ended up in jail. Brian was sentenced to 21 years and she – as a first offender – got 7. With Brian in prison, rumors began to circulate and

Cook got to hear of the relationship; he threatened to kill Brian the next time they met. But Linda, who had refined her charm skills, managed to convince him that he was the only man in her life: otherwise, why would she have had "True love, Ronnie Cook" tattooed on her thigh? At the same time she continued writing to Brian. When she was free once again, in 1989, she visited them both every time it was allowed.

Nonetheless, she secretly feared the day that Ronnie would be back in circulation. He was violent and hot-tempered and not someone you fooled around with. It would be best to get rid of him. She drew up a plan with Brian. He knew a man named Danny Reece, thirty-five years old, in jail for armed robbery. Danny was already infatuated with her, and, for £ 10.000, agreed to be the hit-man. Linda arranged for Cook, who was out on probation the same weekend as Danny, to go with her to her house in King George Avenue.

A Question of Principle

It was a fine late afternoon in November, 1990. The radio was playing *Unchained Melody* by the Righteous Brothers from the sound track of *Ghost*, the most popular film of the decade: an anachronistic note of romanticism to sweeten the punk rock pop that, from Mick Jagger to Madonna, was all the rage in those years.

Ronnie couldn't wait to see his love, to have her all to himself after the years of separation. Waiting to receive him, however, was an unusual butler: Danny Reece, a gun already in hand. But Reece was only a robber, and had never killed anybody. All he did was shoot Cook in the elbow. That was not enough for Linda. She wrenched the gun away from Reece, screamed at Ronnie,

Kneel down!

and shot him in the head. Ronnie died on the spot. The carpet was soaked in blood. Linda told Danny to get away.

Epilogue

The trial finished with a sentence of life in prison, although Linda never once admitted her guilt. According to her version of the facts, the legal battle against the police after the death of her first husband had provoked Scotland Yard into indicting her.

In 1995, in jail, she promised eternal love to Danny, her accomplice. However, in 2009, a year after being released, she married the eccentric Spanish millionaire George Ceasar, seventeen years her senior.

George died in September, 2015. Linda swears that she had nothing to do with this death.

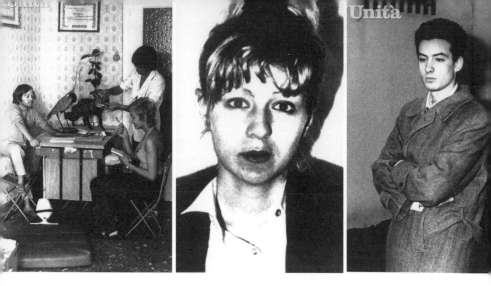

The Dwarf of Termini

Domenico Semeraro (Italy)

"Yes, I killed Domenico Semeraro. I killed him with these hands. He was a disgusting horrible creature. He enslaved me. He didn't deserve to live. He threatened to circulate the photos that he'd taken of me and Michela in certain positions."

The bond between Domenico and Armando was strong. They met in the summer of 1986, when Domenico Semeraro, born in Puglia in 1946, was looking for a handyman for his taxidermy business, and Armando Lovaglio, sixteen and fresh out of school, which he failed, had only one thought in his head: a Honda NSF125.

Large, luminous eyes, superlong eyelashes, small rose-red lips, and a face of mythical legend.

When he opened the door of his workshop on Via Castro Pretorio, in Rome, Semeraro was thunderstruck by the beauty of the young man and quickly wrote it down in his diary.

Only 4 foot 5 tall ("a man in miniature" said Armando), Semeraro loved to surround himself with good-looking young people, and he found them by using job advertisements or by luring them at Termini Station. Armando soon became his favorite. And then something more: the young man was like a God to worship. After a few weeks he gave him the motorcycle he craved, clothes and jewels, and his credit card. They took vacations, sometimes with girls, sometimes with the young boys that hung out with Domenico. They organized parties, and every now and then Domenico even scored some drugs. When Armando was in an accident, Semeraro counterfeited the medical certificate to get insurance compensation so he could buy an even bigger motorcycle.

Inebriated by flattery, it hardly seemed true to Armando that he could be so liked by someone. He began to see in that strange magnetic man a chance for a different future. Domenico knew so many people, and he was always greeted with affection. He could talk to anyone. When Armando's parents began to worry, and tried to stop him from going out with Domenico, Armando left home and moved into the place on Via Castro Pretorio.

Ménage à Trois

In the summer of 1987 Semeraro published a job advertisement to find a secretary. One respondent who showed up was Michela Palazzini: she was sixteen, tall and blond and with a brisk manner. She took Armando's fancy right away. So, a *ménage à trois* was arranged. Desired by both, Armando had never felt so much loved. But while Michela was prepared to share the young man with Domenico, Domenico was jealous, and he coaxed Armando by any means, wanting to keep him all to himself. He would argue:

On the left: Domenico Semeraro and his killers, Michela Palazzini (in the middle) and Armando Lovaglio (on the right).

If you stay a house-husband, even if you to find some proletarian job – in this society you will always count for nothing. (…) You will become ugly, desiccated, emaciated, without that beautiful light in your eyes that illuminates my house. Your future, Armando, should be happy. You'll smile at everyone, wave to everyone from atop an incredible motorcycle, in a beautiful leather jacket, with all these women to dominate as the Dominator.

Armando tried awkwardly to please them both. He would give in to one, but then change his mind. He swore that black was white, but was always caught, exasperating everyone.

The situation became complicated when Michela became pregnant, and she and Armando found an apartment together. Armando continued to go to work for Domenico who, out of desperation, began to threaten and blackmail him. To frighten him, Domenico talked of having melted a man down in the acids. (Nothing has ever been found to substantiate). He threatened to publicize some photographs that he'd taken of them in the intimacy, and boasted about having had an affair with Michela, thus putting the paternity of the child in doubt. At the same time he made Armando more dependent on him: Armando was a heroin addict, and Domenico could get the drug cheap.

The Liberation

On April 25th, 1990, Armando spent all the day at the workshop on Via Castro Pretorio. He did some heroin and began to ride around on the motorcycle; Domenico, meanwhile, showered him with threats, declarations of love, unleashing all the anger that had screamed inside of him for a lifetime. Exasperated, Armando took some more heroin. At 3.00 AM Semeraro was still going full-throttle, and wanted Michela to come over and join them, which the girl immediately did. In the semi-darkness of the room they continued screaming at each other, while dawn began to break outside. Armando moved, and without looking up or say anything passed through a wall of voices, went to the fridge, opened it and flooded the room with light. Domenico seized a scalpel from the workbench and went for Armando's back. "Look out!" Michela screamed. Armando turned and pushed Domenico away. The older man fell to the ground, and Armando got on top of him, his hands tightening around Domenico's neck. Armando was surprised at how weak and submissive the man was. His hands were nearly as large as Domenico's face. He squeezed with all his strength, not moving, for some minutes, until he realized that the small body beneath him had stopped writhing.

The corpse of Domenico Semeraro was found the next morning on the rubbish dump of Corcolle. Some hours later police burst into Armando's parents' house and found the young couple asleep on the divan, in each others arms. Armando confessed to the murder, thus exonerating Michela, who was acquitted as not having committed the crime. Lovaglio was sentenced to 15 years in prison. He served his time in Rebibbia jail.

EXPERT TESTIMONY

According to the famous criminologist and forensic psychiatrist Franco Ferracuti, who was called as an expert witness for the defense of Armando Lovaglio, at the moment Armando attacked Domenico, he was not in a position to understand what he was doing.
Ferracuti regretted that the court itself did not appoint a psychiatric examination. At the end of the trial, he said in an interview with the daily L'Unità: "As a doctor, I am prepared to affirm the mental illness of Lovaglio, irrespective of my role as a defense witness."

Hot for Teacher

Pamela Smart (United States)

It is the evening of May 1st, 1990, and in six days Pamela and Gregory Smart will celebrate their first wedding anniversary. But what greets Pam when she comes back to her home in Derry, New Hampshire, is a jacket soaked in blood, the house turned upside down, and her husband's body. A numbing sequence of thoughts batters the woman's mind. It's like a long drum solo, as in the intro to *Hot for teacher* by Van Halen, Pam's favorite band. A coincidence? Maybe. In any case, in a disconcerting duplication of destinies, the song gives the outlines of one of the most debated and controversial criminal cases in the last few decades: the Smart trial was the first in American history to "benefit" from practically total media coverage.

G regory William Smart first caught Pamela Ann Wojas' eye on December 31st, 1986. Their shared passion for heavy metal and Greg's long hair attracted the girl's attention right away. At the time she was presenting a radio program with the stage name "Maiden of Metal", as she dreamed of a career in show business. On May 1989, Pam and Greg got married and moved to Derry. She worked at the Winnacunnet High School, in Hampton, while he was an insurance agent. However, only seven months after the wedding, Greg was cheated on his wife, and this undermined their relationship.

After the revelation, during a school project, Pam got to know William "Billy" Flynn (fifteen), who was in love with her. To take revenge for her husband's escapade, Pam decided to respond to the boy's attention.

In a short time, what should been a fleeting interlude was transformed into an illicit, intoxicating, and morbid love. In spite of her promises to the boy of life together, Pam refused to ask for a divorce, shattering Billy's dreams.

"If We Want to Go on Seeing Each Other, We'll Need to Get Rid of My Husband"

On the evening of May 1st, 1990, Greg was greeted by a silent home. It was 6 PM and Pam would return later. Crossing the threshold, he found the apartment had been turned upside down. A second later, two boys grabbed him from behind; Billy pointed a .38 caliber at the back of the man's head while his friend, Pete Randall, forced him to his knees. A single shot and Greg collapsed lifeless to the floor. The two boys fled, together with their accomplices Vance Lattime Jr. and Raymond Fowler. When the police arrived, they labeled the crime as a botched burglary. But there was something suspicious.

A few days later, Pete's father handed over a .38 to the police. The net began to close in. Billy, Pete, Vance, and Raymond

---

The young teacher Pamela Wojas Smart.

were interrogated and held by the police, charged with man-slaughter. The four pointed to the teacher as the brain of the plan, and decided to cooperate.

At the same time, a tip-off led to Cecilia Pierce, Pam's intern. The girl declared that she knew of a plan to get rid of Greg:

Pam is seeing Billy, but the fear of losing everything has stopped her from asking for a divorce . . . I know that this makes Billy mad.

These declarations gave the police a plausible motive, which deepened their first suspicions of the teacher.

The Girl of Ice

In court, the burden of his actions was too much for Billy. In tears, he admitted to killing Greg under Pamela's cool pressure.

By phone taps, the police also managed to obtain a half-confession from Pam:

If they had kept their mouth shut, it would've been the perfect crime.

Supported by the four boys' statements, that statement, not even particularly veiled, persuaded the investigators to issue an arrest warrant.

On August 1st, 1990, detective Pelletier burst into the school: "Pam, I have some good news and some bad news. The good news is that we've solved the case. The bad news is that you're under arrest."

When Pamela entered the courtroom for the first time, public opinion had already expressed its verdict. The woman immediately confessed to her affair with Billy, but during the whole trial she declared her innocence with cold detachment. Never a tear, no remorse. This behavior earned her the nickname "Girl of Ice", and was interpreted by most people as proof of her ruthlessness.

For Pam, her longed-for popularity turned out to be a mockery. On March 22nd, 1991, in a dazzling explosion of flashbulbs, she was sentenced to life in prison without parole.

The four boys negotiated a plea bargain and were imprisoned. Vance and Raymond were freed in 2005. Pete and Billy were released on parole in early 2015.

Pamela Smart is serving her sentence in Bedford Hills maximum-security prison, New York. With the support of her family, she continues to proclaim her innocence. Only a new version of the truth provided by Billy might free the teacher who seduced her pupil.

IN FRONT OF THE TELEVISION CAMERAS

During the trial, the presence television cameras in the courtroom made the case into a spectacle: according to those who believe in her innocence, the atmosphere of general voyeurism influenced the jurors' judgment. Moreover, at the beginning of the trial the ex-intern Cecilia Pierce sold the rights to her story for $ 100.000. The case has inspired two films, various documentaries, and numerous publications.

This visibility also extends to the web. On the homepage of the site Pamelasmart.com, this sentence stands out: "Who wouldn't support a woman who still wears the Scarlet Letter and is hated by an unforgiving public that has been fed poison and lies by the media for 25 years?" This question was posed by Eleanor Pam, Pamela's psychiatrist and supporter, who has organized a petition to reopen the case.

SPORTS ★ ★ ★ FINAL

JAIL DEAL SAVES STRAWBERRY CAREER

EXCLUSIVE IN SPORTS

DAILY NEWS

SEVENTY-FIVE YEARS · JUNE 26, 1919

50¢   NEW YORK'S HOMETOWN NEWSPAPER   Friday, January 27, 1995

O.J. SAYS HE'LL ALWAYS WONDER:

WHAT DID SHE THINK AT THE END?

SIMPSON SAYS HE WOULD HAVE PROTECTED NICOLE – PAGES 2 & 3

An American Tragedy

O. J. Simpson (United States)

Money, fame, success. Media exposure, racial and sexual conflicts. The rise and eclipse of a champion: a controversial trial that leaves many questions open. And then, these other problems with the law . . .

June 13th, 1994. 10.15 PM. The Brentwood district of Los Angeles. A dog wanders in the road barking plaintively, dragging its leash behind it. It has blood on its legs. A passerby sees it, makes sure that it is not injured, and leaves it with a friend to look after. Around midnight, this friend takes it for a walk and is led toward a nearby villa. At the entrance, behind a white gate, lie two tortured, lifeless bodies.

The police, called by the man, discovers that the dead are Nicole Brown, the owner of the dog and the former wife of the football champion O. J. Simpson, and Ron Goldman, a waiter in a nearby restaurant. They had died after being stabbed tens of times.

The first suspect is Simpson, and a few days later he is asked to appear at the police station. At 11 AM on June 17th more than thousand journalists – he is a famous figure – are there waiting for him. But in vain. At 5 PM his attorney reads a letter suggesting an imminent suicide:

I have nothing to do with the murder of Nicole. Don't worry about me. I've had a wonderful life.

An hour and twenty minutes later, however, a motorist sees Simpson driving his white Ford Bronco. He informs the police.

O. J. Simpson murder case on the front page of Daily News *on January 27th, 1995.*

Twenty police cars and twenty helicopters begin the chase. All the media interrupt their programs to broadcast images of the pursuit live: 95 million people stay glued to their televisions on the big three networks (ABC, CBS and NBC) and on CNN. The shops selling pizza deliveries do a roaring trade. At 8 PM, after reaching his mother's house and talking with her for an hour, Simpson gives himself up to the authorities.

A Wonderful Life

O. J. Simpson met Nicole, an attractive eighteen-year-old blond girl, in 1977, in the nightclub *The Daisy*, where she was working as a waitress. Even though he was married, they started to go out together. In 1985, as soon as he had divorced his first wife, the couple got married, moved into an exclusive district, and in a short time had two children, Sydney and Justin.

After seven years, and repeated reports by Nicole of physical abuse, they divorced. O. J. had already had problems with the law: in his youth, when he was a member of the street gang Persian Warriors, he briefly spent time in a reform school in San Francisco, the city where he was born on July 9th, 1947. Then, following tremendous success in sports, he became a celebrity: in 1973, when he played for the Buffalo Bills, he was named as Best Player in the NFL, the American professional football league. When he retired, he held many records: few could match him in receiving, running the ball down the field, or in scoring.

Simpson was also at his ease on the set, making numerous commercials as well as films for the small and large screen: the three films in the series *The Naked Gun* were very successful.

The third episode was released in theaters a few months before the double homicide. All in all, he was a perfect example of the American Dream – up to that evening.

What Happened That Evening?

The trial commenced on January 24th, 1995, judge Lance Ito presiding. Simpson, in what was called the crime of the century, was defended by a team of some of the most successful attorneys in America (among them were two specialists in DNA evidence), led first by Robert Shapiro and then by Johnnie Cochran. The grand total of all the fees: between $ 3 and $ 6 million. Of the twelve jurors, ten were women and nine were African-Americans. The racial question certainly counted: a few months before, *Time* had published a photo of Simpson on its cover, with the caption

An American Tragedy.

When the same shot appeared on the cover of *Newsweek*, readers quickly noticed that *Time*'s cover was darker: a graphic artist had made the face blacker to, so to speak, make it more threatening.

The defense wanted to convince the jury that Simpson was a victim of justice, and that the murder could be linked to an outstanding question of drugs. The prosecution presented – even in the absence of a murder weapon and witnesses – a very different story.

Nicole, on the evening of June 12th, after putting the children to bed, had opened their front door and been attacked by her ex-husband, who brutally stabbed her before she could cry out.

A short time before she had called the restaurant where she had dined that evening, asking whether they could bring by some glasses which her mother had left there. Thus, as she was dying, Ron Goldman arrived: maybe he rushed to help her. He was killed in turn. The murderer then gave the *coup de grâce:* raising her head by the hair, he cut her carotid artery. The defense and prosecution were in agreement that all this happened between 10.15 and 11.40 PM. Simpson had been last seen, with his bodyguard, at 9.36 PM, after eating a hamburger in a fast food restaurant. He then reappeared at 10.54 PM (when he greeted the driver of the limousine that was to take him to the airport to fly to Chicago).

Cochran stated candidly that his client was sleeping at the time of the murder; moreover, because he suffered from a strong form of arthritis, the defendant would not have been able to physically overcome Goldman, an athletic young man who had strenuously defended himself.

The Verdict

It was feared that riots would break out in the city, as they did three years before, after the acquittal of the police officers responsible for the brutal beating of the Afro-American taxi driver Rodney King. All the police of the city were on duty. A hundred mounted police surrounded the courtroom. President Bill Clinton was continuously updated.

Once more, the entire nation was glued to the television: long-distance calls decreased by 58%, New York Stock Exchange dealings by 41%. Even water consumption decreased. In fact, the media followed the case in every detail: the *Los*

Angeles Times, for example, had something on the front page for 10 months. Sony and IBM received free and unexpected publicity: their logos were in full sight on the portable computers used by judge Ito, who from time to time sipped Diet Coke. After more than 8 months of hearings, during which 150 witnesses were heard, on the morning of October 3rd, 1995, the jurors expressed the succinct verdict:

Not guilty.

The decisive factors were the errors committed in the course of investigations by members of the Los Angeles Police Department, as well as some racist remarks made by a key investigator, whose conduct cost him credibility. Furthermore, DNA tests in those years were relatively new and thus considered less accurate than they are today: a trace of Nicole's blood was discovered on a sock found in Simpson's residence; there was O. J.'s blood on the left glove found at the crime scene.

A witness even related that in the minutes after the murder, he had seen the Ford Bronco driving away from the crime scene, barely missing another car; another witness, a

O. J. SIMPSON IN PRISON

Two years after the criminal verdict, a jury found Simpson guilty at the conclusion of the civil suit started by the family of the victims, obliging him to pay $ 33.5 million in damages.
In 2008, O. J. Simpson was sentenced to 33 years in prison for a casino robbery carried out on the night of September 13th, 2007, with accomplices in the Palace Station Hotel in Las Vegas: among the charges were also armed robbery and kidnapping. He is serving the sentence in the Lovelock Correctional Center in Nevada. On his dark blue uniform is the number 1027820.

shop owner, said that at the end of May he had sold Simpson a German-made knife with a 11,8 inches blade, which was compatible with the victims' wounds. Nicole, in a 911 telephone call played to the jury by the prosecution, had said she feared that her ex-husband could harm her. Near Nicole's lifeless body was a footprint from a Bruno Magli shoe, in Simpson's exact size: a photographer found an old photograph showing O. J. wearing that extremely expensive model, of which there were only few pairs in the United States. At O. J.'s home the right glove was found, even though in court it did not seem to be the defendant's size. Cochran cleverly seized the opportunity, inflicting the decisive blow on the prosecution:

If those gloves don't fit him, you must acquit him!

Simpson, immortalized smiling and satisfied, was a free man.

The Poisoned Josacine

Jean Marc Deperrois (France)

On June 11th, 1994, the village of Gruchet-le-Valasse is celebrating a medieval festival. Émilie Tanay, nine years old, has come in from a nearby village to take part in the night's festivities. Without warning, the child collapses. She dies a few hours later. It would be discovered that an antibiotic (Josacine) Émilie had taken contained a massive dose of cyanide. But who would want the death of the child? The trial, controversial and hotly contested, led to the condemnation of Jean-Marc Deperrois, a man well known and respected. Émilie may have been an innocent victim, the mistaken target of a crime of passion. Not everybody accepts this theory.

C aux is a remote area of the Haut-Normandie region in northern France. Its inhabitants are distant, often closed, like the area itself. But in Gruchet-le-Valasse (3000 inhabitants) all is in ferment for the medieval night. Émilie Tanay, in her court jester costume, is excited about the festivities and because she is the guest of the Tocquevilles, the family of her friend Jérôme. Her mother, Corinne Tanay, has given this couple (acquaintances of hers) a bottle of Josacine, the antibiotic that Émilie is taking for her bronchitis. At 8 PM, the child swallows her medicine without protest; she only remarks on the unpleasant taste and runs into the kitchen to rinse out her mouth. Then, with the others, she heads happily towards the car. Suddenly, a tremor shakes the child and she falls to the ground in strange convulsions. She is rushed to the hospital in Le Havre, but when her parents arrive she is already dead. The inexplicable death is attributed at first to natural causes.

The Nearly Perfect Crime

Only later was the bottle of Josacine examined: the laboratory analysis found traces of cyanide in it. Cyanide is a powerful poison which is dispersed quickly in the body: it is difficult to procure and a perfect method for murder.

As is always the case when children are victims of a crime, the parents were the prime suspects. The Tanays were very disturbed by the violence of the insinuations, and by police custody. Their lives were subjected to microscopic examination: their money problems, old family feuds, tensions with his parents. They got no support from people in the area, who considered the couple a little outlandish.

After a few days investigators turned up something of interest: Jérôme's mother, Sylvie Tocqueville, who worked as a secretary for the mayor, admitted to having had a relationship with Jean-Marc Deperrois, the deputy mayor and owner of a company that produced industrial thermographs. Under interrogation, both ad-

A woman showing the picture of the little Émilie Tanay during the trial (on the left); on the right: Jean Marc Deperrois in handcuffs.

mitted that there had been some kisses, caresses, and that they had slept together, but only once. In any case, the affair was practically history. Practically. The situation described by witnesses was very different. They spoke of Jean-Marc as being obsessed with his coy lover, of stalking her hoping that her husband, Jean-Michel, might step out for a few hours; they spoke of threats of divorce, angry scenes, and intimidation. But betrayal is not a crime. The suspicions arose from a telephone recording of June 22nd: it was discovered that Deperrois had acquired a kilo of cyanide some weeks before. At first he denied this. Then he claimed that he had bought it for experiments at work. For fear of being accused, he had gotten rid of it by throwing it into the Seine, and for the same reason he had not mentioned it to the investigators. On June 16th, however, the day he had gotten rid of the poison, nobody had known that the substance that killed Émilie was cyanide.

What happened was presented as a crime of passion: Deperrois, after trying to convince Sylvie to leave her husband, decided to intervene personally. Jean-Michel, a delicate hypochondriac, unwittingly supplied the perfect cover for the crime. Moreover, the office of the mayor lay between the Tocquevilles residence and the Deperrois company. A few meters walk, and Deperrois, on June 11th, could have entered the house by the French window undisturbed, and added the poison to the bottle of antibiotic that was standing in full view on the drawing-room table and that he believed was meant for his rival.

A Respected Man

Deperrois was arrested on July 27th. The news upset the county. Nobody wanted to believe that such a respectable man was guilty. Anne-Marie, the betrayed wife, defended her husband without ever showing the slightest hesitation. Sylvie Tocqueville described such conjectures as absurd. Not even the alleged rival, Jean-Michel, believed that he had been the intended victim. Even the press sided with the deputy mayor. Only the Tanays, in the silence that they offered as a defense against the gossip and accusations, reserved their judgment.

It took three years and tens of thousands of pages of transcript to reach a verdict: Jean-Marc Deperrois was declared guilty and condemned to 20 years in prison. The man continued strenuously to claim he was the victim of a miscarriage of justice. In 2006, after 12 years in prison, he was granted freedom on condition that he made no public statement about the affair for three years.

THE COUNTER-INQUIRY

After the trial, Anne-Marie Deperrois set up a committee in support of her husband, and continued to champion the cause of his innocence. In 2003, Jean-Michel Dumay, a journalist for Le Monde, published a book in which he put forward the theory of a domestic accident, which was then disguised by adding cyanide to the antibiotic.

In support of this theory was a mysterious phone call of June 16th, 1994, in which a friend of Jean-Michel Tocqueville's refers to a substance he added to the Josacine. By mistake the child swallowed a product made up of cyanide left unattended by the Tocquevilles. Jean-Michel, who remained at home with the bottle while the child was taken to the hospital, could have added poison to the antibiotic at that point. In fact, nothing unusual was noticed on the arrival of the paramedics while, when the bottle was examined again some hours later, it gave off an unmistakable smell of ammonia.

Page 6 Girl

Julie Scully (Greece)

There's something about a cruise. For the young Greek man, Georgios, it was his first as the ship's chief engineer. For the attractive American model, Julie, it represented an attempt at reconciliation with her husband. Their chance meeting led to a sudden, turbulent relationship – which foundered because of the man's violent jealousy.

S he was lovely. She was the most beautiful woman that Georgios Skiadopoulos had ever seen. He was enchanted when he saw her walking along the corridor of the *Galaxy*, the Celebrity Cruises ship which sailed that evening, November 1st, 1997, on a tour of the Caribbean. It was his first day at work as chief engineer. He was born on July 24th, 1974, in Kavàla, a little town on the north-east coast of Greece, and he'd always wanted to go to sea. Yet seeing the girl cancelled every other emotion: he absolutely had to get to know her.

The opportunity presented itself the following morning, and it was love at first sight. Julie Scully was from the United States. She was six years older than he was; she was a model, and she lived in a magnificent house in Mansfield Township in New Jersey. The mother of Katie, a little girl of two, she was unsatisfied with her second husband, Tim, who wouldn't demonstrate affection in ways she wanted him to. Georgios and Julie spent an intense week's cruise, indifferent to the oblivious husband, who had sailed with Julie in an attempt to mend a marriage in crisis.

The vacation ended, but Julie and Georgios could not be without each other. They thus began to exchange passionate

Greek police escorting Georgios Skiadopoulos.

letters and long phone calls. The desire to see each other again was so strong that Georgios managed to persuade her to sail again on the *Galaxy*, on February 13th, 1998. This time, as well, Tim's presence did not prevent the two lovers from enjoying every moment together. Then on June 19th, in Vancouver, Julie embarked on the same ship not as a tourist, but as the engineer's girlfriend. Meanwhile, Tim learned about the relationship and had asked for a divorce. Georgios and the beautiful American began to program their new life together.

Two Restless Personalities

The lovers had a difficult childhood in common. Georgios was the son of a fisherman who often had to work far from home. He couldn't stand an exclusively female household, and felt shaken because his father had definitively abandoned him. He began to show symptoms of a schizophrenic disorder, one time going so far as to attack and almost to kill his father.

Julie, for her part, had been abandoned by her father at the age of eight and had grown-up with a violent, unsatisfied and constantly drugged mother. Julie also began to take drugs: the vice was needed to alleviate an overwhelming sense of restlessness.

Georgios and Julie were in love: she was at the center of his attention, and he was very possessive of his amazing girlfriend. Nothing would frustrate their desire for a happy future together. After a brief, carefree vacation at Kavàla, Julie moved to Greece on December 6th.

However, very soon, the idyll seemed to fade. Julie suffered greatly from her distance from her daughter, whom she had not been allowed to bring with her, and was nostalgic for her comfortable life in New Jersey. Life in Greece wasn't as satisfying as she had imagined it would be. Georgios noticed his beloved's constant moodiness and began to fear he would lose her. In time, he became more and more intolerant of wife's dissatisfaction. There were frequent arguments, which culminated in an extremely violent episode: Georgios took Julie by the throat. Two months before, he'd done the same thing to Julie's mother. From that evening on, Julie began to fear for her safety.

A Brief Truce

On January 3rd, 1999, it seemed that calm had returned. Georgios organized a party for his fiancée's 31st birthday, and everything went well. He was about to leave for his military service, which would keep him away from home for two years, and this led them to make a decision: they would get married in a few days. And while her husband was away, Julie would return to America to be with Katie. It was the best solution for everyone.

On January 8th they got into the car and left for Athens, where they would apply for a marriage license. But during the journey the fears and insecurity assailing both of them emerged again.

ON THE COVER

In her early twenties, Julie became quite famous locally because of some photos of her published on the famous Page 6 of the *Trentonian*, which showed beautiful girls in bikinis. In fact, it was the same New Jersey paper that stirred people into action regarding Julie's disappearance by putting the story on the front page. And when public opinion took interest in the case, the Greek authorities expedited their enquiries.

At the mere idea of losing his Julie, Georgios panicked and pulled over. Suddenly, he grabbed the woman by her throat. There was no one there to stop him. Julie died without being able to embrace her little girl again.

Georgios found a secluded place and parked the car. With gasoline, he tried to set the body on fire, but rain prevented him from carrying out this plan. So he tried to hide the corpse in a suitcase, but it was too small. Thus he decapitated his beloved's body, threw the suitcase into a pond and her head into the sea . . . The currents would take it out to sea.

Georgios pretended that Julie had disappeared without a trace. He reported the disappearance to the Greek police and the American embassy. The model's mysterious disappearance piqued the interest of the media, especially American. Georgios was interviewed several times, and inaccuracies in his accounts betrayed him. He was summoned by investigators and, after an intensive interrogation studded with inconsistencies, he gave in. On December 6th, 2000, he was sentenced to life in prison.

False Identities

Thomas Montgomery (United States)

It was a virtual relationship with extreme consequences. In upstate New York, far from the City, Thomas Montgomery's bored life is suddenly rejuvenated by a mind-blowing online adventure. A love that resulted in jealousy for a woman, Jessi, he never actually meets, and ended with the death of Brian, a colleague and friend of him in real life.

A low yellow light came from the kitchen, but Cindy was already in bed. The two children had also been sleeping for a while. Thomas, however, wasn't sleepy. Beyond his square-lens glasses a light on the screen of the computer flashed the score of the poker game in progress. He was losing, as usual, and he couldn't stop. It was early May, and the first signs of spring had begun to show in Clarence.

Suddenly a dialog box appeared: "Talhotblond wants to chat with you." He had subscribed to the site to play online poker, but he had never used the chat feature before. The name was inviting; was she really tall and blond? He clicked "Accept". Jessi, as she called herself, sent a photo. She was in a swimsuit, and not only tall and blond but rather provocative: a luminous smile, just about eighteen.

Thomas was dumbfounded for a moment, uncertain about what to do, his finger poised motionless over the mouse. He was forty-seven years old, married for ten years, worked all his life: it weighed him down. He looked up and saw himself in a photo taken seventeen years before, when he was in the armed forces: in a white hat, he was proud to wear the uniform. In a sudden surge of excitement he began to write: his nickname was "marinesniper" and from that moment on for Jessi he was Tommy: thirty years old, six feet tall, muscular, and just back from Iraq.

In a short time, the virtual correspondence became more real than real life. Jessi and Tommy exchanged photos and intimacies, declarations of affection, and soon enough they were having uninhibited cyber-sex at all hours of the day.

I will always love you, Tommy, wrote Jessi.

I have never felt anything so strong, he replied.

They started a correspondence. He'd write her from Clarence, in upstate New York, and she'd respond from Oak Hill, West Virginia. She sent him sexy lingerie.

Thomas maintained the fiction better than he could have imagined. He woke up early to take the dog for a walk and to open in secret these packages addressed to him. To divert his wife's suspicions, he justified them with a surprise for their anniversary. Thomas talked about his virtual relationship with his colleagues at work, and in the locker room after exercise. His friends envied him a little for his success with this sweet blond.

Thomas Montgomery wearing the military uniform at thirty (on the left), and at forty-seven (in the middle); on the right: Brian Barrett.

A Family Photo

Feminine intuition is not easily fooled, however. Cindy was not convinced by the facile explanations of her husband, and the umpteenth package provoked her curiosity. So it was that she discovered the "affair", read the exchanges in chat, and listened secretly to phone calls. She also wrote a letter to Jessi, telling the truth. She attached a family photo.

> Let me introduce you to these people. The man you see in the center of the photo is Tom, my husband since 1989. He is forty-seven years old.

Jessi was astounded. She had never expected it. She sent her virtual lover a very strong message; their relationship had to end. All of the fictitious feelings they'd mistook for real ones were shattered into fragments in an instant.

Partly for revenge, partly because of her need to continue the dangerous game they'd both become dependent on, she contacted Brian Barrett, a colleague of Thomas', asking him to confirm what she had been told. Brian, twenty-two years old, invented nothing, neither about the real life of his friend nor anything about himself: he was a student at SUNY Buffalo, and worked part-time in the same metal and mechanics factory as Thomas. He was a good looking young man in the flower of his youth. He was definitely more attractive to Jessi, who immediately became intimate and affectionate with him, not at all put off by how badly the first affair had ended. They fixed an appointment to meet the very next weekend. They hadn't considered just how furiously possessive Thomas might be.

Reality is Different

Initially, Thomas tried to be reasonable. He had a beautiful family, after all. He had been taking a risk with this affair, and in fact he'd been all too ready to lose his head over a pair of blue eyes. But real life was something else and he had a lot to be grateful for.Still, he couldn't accept that all the bragging talk with friends and colleagues was over. And when he realized that Brian and Jessi were serious, he went into a blind rage of pride mixed with jealousy.

Brian will pay in blood,

he wrote, in one of his last messages to Jessi.

On the evening of September 15th, 2006, Thomas put on his cammies, as if to go hunting: he wanted to go back to being the "marinesniper" of the chatline, to show that snotty-nosed kid who the real warrior was. He loaded the gun in his van and set off

A DOCUMENTARY AND A FILM

In 2009 the story of Thomas, Jessi and Brian inspired the documentary *Talhotblond*, written and directed by the Emmy Award-Winning journalist Barbara Schroeder. Thomas Montgomery and some of Brian's relatives, as well as various participants in the case, from the clinical psychologist, lawyers, and the Erie County Sheriff all appear in the documentary. In the year of its release, *Talhotblond* received an award at the Seattle International Film Festival.

The documentary also inspired the film, *Tall Hot Blonde* (2012), made for TV and directed by Courteney Cox, who plays the role of confidant to Thomas' wife in the film. The cast includes Garret Dillahunt, Brando Eaton, and Laura San Giacomo, well-known stars from many TV series and small screen productions.

for the factory in Buffalo. He crouched, waiting in the car park. As soon as the evening shift ended, Brian came out and got into his car. He was sitting in the driver's seat, his cell phone in hand, when he was hit by three .30 caliber bullets fired from point blank range. The next morning someone noticed a corpse in the car.

The investigation was rather fast: the connections with Thomas were so numerous and obvious that the Buffalo police were soon knocking on Thomas' door, ready to take him away in handcuffs. At about the same time, police went to Jessi's home in Oak Hill. Some clarification was required of the blond femme fatale who united victim and executioner. The investigators were as astonished as Thomas. The fingers which had struck sweet effusions from the keyboard and created unspeakable erotic dreams for these men were those of Mary Shieler, forty-five, with two daughters. Jessi was the name of one of the adolescents, and the photos that had been sent were of her, who naturally was in the dark about everything. But Thomas and Brian were not Mary's only conquests: the housewife was accustomed to provoking and seducing men online, men she didn't have to face in real life. For the more explicit virtual appointments she had also used her daughter, secretly aiming the webcam beneath her skirt.

Thomas Montgomery was sentenced to 20 years for murder. He is serving his time in New York's Attica Prison. Mary Shieler, though she flouted every moral standard, did not actually do anything illegal. The daughters broke off all contact with her after that; and her relationship with her husband has also suffered. He has asked for a divorce.

The most disturbing thing about the story was that, of the main actors of the affair, the only one to tell the truth was Brian.

The Devout Murderer

Gerardo Rocha Vera (Chile)

His much-proclaimed devotion to St. Thomas Aquinas did not prevent him from killing his rival in love. And it did not even save him from the consequences of his act. Thus the greatest proprietor of private schools in Chile, the enormously wealthy Gerardo Rocha Vera, out of jealousy, killed and burned Jaime Oliva, losing his own life in the fire he started.

H e himself theorized, "One can't have everything in life." And to try and justify himself: "I have written a book on forgiveness to achieve happiness. I have never achieved it." His devotion to St. Thomas Aquinas, after whom he named the university he founded, did not protect him from his passions. Gerardo Rocha was a powerful man in Chile. Beginning in 1987, he created a private educational system founded on technical institutes, colleges, and universities. 50 thousand students attended his schools. The network had been extended to other countries:

Bolivia, Ethiopia, Vietnam, and Mozambique. The value of Rocha's International Council amounted to about $ 80 million.

Signs from Long Ago

He married Carla Haardt when he was very young. They had two children. One day he discovered that an old classmate had gifted his wife a purse. Mad with jealousy, he pummeled the other man. Then he went home, beat his wife, and burned the present, which he considered an insult. The marriage of the young, devoutly Catholic couple went up in smoke together with the purse.

In the 1990s, Jaime Oliva was the director of court auctions in Santiago. One day Rocha went to see him to ask a favor. Very soon he fell in love with Oliva's young secretary, Veronica Espinosa, who was 10 years younger. They got married. While the business was booming, the couple had three children. But in Rocha's brain, the worm of jealousy worked away: he was convinced that in the past there had been a relationship between Veronica and Jaime, who was now retired. So he started to plan his revenge.

Crime in the Sanctuary of Vacation

On the evening of February 21st, 2008, Rocha went with two accomplices to Oliva's home, in the seaside resort of El Quisco, upon the pretext of renting the house for his holiday. But as soon as they got in, they killed Oliva, and then, to destroy the evidence, set the house on fire. But an unexpected explosion ripped the building to shreds, and Rocha was lost in the flames.

The accomplices managed to escape, but nothing could be done for the "devout murderer". He had burns over 42% of his body. His agony was long and relentless, and in May of that year he died. Even saints have their dark side.

Gerardo Rocha Vera, killed by his own uncontrollable jealousy.

In the Eyes of Travis

Jodi Arias (United States)

The car she left with from California, one warm week in June, wasn't the car she ended up in, a few days later, in Utah. The fast trip, loaded with self-aggrandizement and anger, had one objective: to win back a man's love.

Yreka, California. Dawn, June 2nd, 2008. Jodi Arias gets into her car and by 8 AM she's already in Redding, on the road to Sacramento.

Besides her striking oxygenated hair and a smile that radiates in all the selfies on her MySpace profile, Jodi has a sharp, resolute air. Her emotional situation, apparently linear, in reality flips through different planes. There's Darryl, her former fiancé, former cohabitant, present friend but within undefined borders. And there's Ryan, new flame, maybe a new boyfriend. And there's Travis. The relationship with Travis Alexander (thirty-one years old), a Mormon, officially ended a couple of months ago. But, unknown to Ryan, Jodi and Travis continue to see each other.

Jodi is on the road to meet Ryan in West Jordan, Utah, where he lives. Before leaving, she tells Darryl that she'll see him in Monterey. When she arrives in Redding, the young woman leaves her car at her sister's house and rents another at the airport. The official reason is the gas-mileage: the trip will be long. Jodi drives alone for mile after mile through California, stopping only to fill up. In Salinas, below San Francisco, she takes a longer break, at a hairdressing salon. She is in Buckeye, Arizona, late in morning on June 3rd.

The girl next door look of Jody Arias during the trial.

She meets Ryan, falling into his arms, in Utah only on the afternoon of the 5th.

Monday, June 9th

The body of Travis Alexander was found on June 9th, in his apartment in Mesa, Arizona. Travis was naked, slumped over in the shower: he'd been ferociously stabbed twenty-nine times and shot point-blank range in the face, just under his right eye. His throat was cut, from ear to ear. There was blood everywhere: on the bathroom floor, on the walls, in the sink.

The police found a digital camera in the washing machine. It looked like blood stained clothes had been recently washed. Travis' computer and cell phone revealed that there had been no internet connection in the previous five days.

The death of the young man surprised everyone. A good boy, said his family. Reliable, great worker, religious, no bad friends. He had some girlfriends, recently a new one. Before her, there'd been Jodi.

On the 4th, Travis seemed to have vanished into thin air. Jodi had phoned him on the 5th and left some messages on the machine. She'd also sent an email, writing that she would not be able to pick him up on her way to West Jordan.

When the girl arrived in Mesa, she looked different: she had brown hair and a pair of light glasses that hid a surprisingly modest look.

Three Fortuitous Snaps

It was a handful of photos, a hat, and a fingerprint off the left hand that drew attention to Jodi.

The camera found in the washing machine turned out to be a key element in the investigation. Some photos had been deleted, but they were recovered from the memory card that had survived the washing. But there were others photos found in the machine, as well: Jodi and Travis naked together in bed. Then there was Travis in the shower with his eyes closed and his head slightly inclined under the jet of water; and finally the young man looked into the lens, an air of resignation in the expression. The shot was dated June 4th. Taken at 5.29 PM, it was the last of Travis alive. There followed three photos that seemed to be taken accidentally: one was completely out of focus (5.30 PM), another framed the ceiling of the bathroom (5.31 PM), and the third was of the profusely bleeding body of a man. It was a dark and grainy photo, but the slashed corpse could be recognized as Travis'.

Forensic analysis results showed that the bloodstained print and the hat which were found at the scene of the crime were Jodi's. And what gradually emerged from testimony by Travis' close friends completed the picture.

Jodi and Travis had met two years before, during a convention in Las Vegas. The attraction between them was very strong. Jodi was overwhelmed. Above all, she took the affair very seriously. The relationship quickly appeared lopsided: she wanted at all costs to be part of Travis' life. She committed herself to becoming a Mormon, and in November, 2006, Travis himself baptized her. She moved to Mesa, where he lived.

Travis, on the other hand, felt embattled, annoyed by the insistence of the girl. Jodi's lack of sexual scruples both attracted and repelled him. When he began to feel hunted, he had ended the affair; still, he and Jodi continued to meet, in secret, to have sex. In April, 2008, she returned to Yreka, to live with her grandparents. But she seemed not to have accepted the end of the relationship. She was obsessed with Travis and was becoming more and more invasive. She managed to hack into his email account, his MySpace profile, and his online checking account. When she discovered that he was going with another girl, her obsession had become uncontrollable.

She turned up at his apartment unannounced. She snuck into the place, to spy on the two while they slept. She punctured the tires of their cars many times. His friends, alarmed, put him on guard.

Jodi's (Changing) Version

Even when the evidence collected by the police clearly pointed at her, Jodi would not surrender: with febrile stubbornness she prepared her bags and loaded the car for another long trip. She was about to start the motor when the police blocked her way. They handcuffed her. It was July 15th.

The investigators described Jodi as an unpredictable, capricious person: sometimes she was meek, sometimes uncontrollable. She was filmed by security cameras in a room at Siskiyou County prison, where she was taken after her arrest, while she waited for the detective. The film was amazing: the girl laughed, did a vertical jump on the wall, talked to herself in a high voice, sang Dido's *Here with me*.

In the beginning Jodi categorically denied being in Mesa or having met Travis on June 4th: she said that she was driving towards West Jordan on that day. Then, under the incessant pressure of the investigators, she changed her version.

She admitted being at the apartment of her ex, and she admitted being present at the time of the murder, but denied committing it. She said that two people – a man and a woman – disguised as ninjas broke into the apartment, killed Travis, and threatened to kill her if she revealed the fatal attack to anyone. The story was too Hollywood to be credible, but Jodi managed to repeat it over and over for the first two years she spent in prison, waiting for the trial.

Then, without warning, an about-face: she admitted to having murdered Travis, but claimed she couldn't remember any details of the homicide. The defense psychiatrist, Dr. Samuels,

MEDIA OBSESSION

The Arias trial, begun on December 10th, 2012, in Maricopa County, was the object of maximum media focus. The American public followed it like a "reality show". Opposing "guilty" and "innocent" factions fought ferocious virtual battles on social networks. On YouTube there were computer simulated reconstructions of the competing hypotheses of the dynamics of the crime. CNN created a streaming channel exclusively dedicated to the trial. When the photos found in Travis' digital camera were put online, the morbid interest of the public reached unheard of peaks.

Even inside the courtroom the public was out of control. A reporter for USA Today described surrealistic scenes: people screaming, a cell phone that sounded like a braying ass that kept interrupted one hearing, and a woman who vomited off the gallery. The messages posted online against Jodi gradually became more numerous and heavy, and the "innocent" faction began to lose ground – though without ever admitting defeat. One of the web sites dedicated to supporting the girl posted a blowup of the image of Travis' right eye. It was taken from the last photo that showed him alive: some claimed to see, reflected in the pupil, the shadowy outline of two figures, armed and apparently disguised as ninjas . . .

described this declaration as illustrating a post-traumatic stress disorder in which a tragic event can inhibit memory. It was a case of dissociative amnesia.

After four years in jail, Jodi made a last-ditch effort: she seemed to repent, and confessed to being forced to kill Travis in legitimate self-defense. In support of this thesis her lawyers produced in evidence some letters that demonstrated the physical and psychological submission of Jodi to her lover. Jodi recounted an erotic game they'd played on that June 4th: Travis had tied her to the bed with a rope, and then used a long kitchen knife to cut the bonds. She had taken some photos while he was in the shower.

Then something happened that seemed banal: the camera slipped from her hand, and fell, and Travis had become furious. He jumped on her and, screaming at her, knocked her hard against the wall. He chased her all over the apartment. Jodi, terrorized, scrambled up on a stool to get the gun that he kept on a shelf. She begged him to stop. But he wouldn't listen – so she shot him. Travis fell down injured, but managed to get up continue pursuing her. At that point the girl defended herself with the knife found on the floor by the bed. But then the man finally collapsed in the bathroom. Jodi said she had no recollection of even one drop of blood.

Homicidal Fury

This new version of the facts, with poor Jodi as the victim of perfidious Travis' repeated abuse, triggered a prolonged battle of scientific analyses, expert witnesses, simulations, testimony and confrontations.

The evidence was for the most part against Jodi, and revealed an obvious attempt by the defense to mystify of the facts. The letters produced by the defense were shown to be false. No trace of rope was found in the apartment, and in any case there was no part of Travis' bed to which it could have been tied. The brutality of the blows, and the variety of the weapons used, suggested a homicidal fury that had nothing to do with self-defense. And the dynamics of the aggression reconstructed by Jodi leaked water everywhere. According to the experts, if she had shot him before using the knife, the shot would have either killed Travis instantly or rendered him completely incapable of reacting. Finally, there was the spent cartridge: the police found it on top of Travis' clotted blood. This meant that the shot had been fired after the man was stabbed, not before. It was a .25 caliber cartridge, the same caliber as a gun that went mysteriously missing the month before from Jodi's grandparents' house in Yreka. The gun was never found.

The prosecution tore Jodi's account to shreds and recomposed the crime from a completely different perspective: Jodi had brought the gun and knife from Yreka; Jodi had hit Travis in the back while he was in the shower, and then stabbed him in the heart, the chest, and the side while he tried to parry the knife blows. She stabbed him in the back as he staggered toward the bathroom sink. Then Travis tried to escape, limping into the bedroom. But there, on the threshold, Jodi cut his throat from ear to ear. Then she dragged him into the bathroom and shot him.

A Bunch of Violet Irises

As she had already partially admitted, Jodi first tried to remove traces of the murder. Then she tried to mislead the investigation. Shortly after the crime she put the bloodstained clothes into the washing machine; she put the knife in dishwasher; she changed the license plates on her car to try and erase any trace of her stop-over in Mesa. She switched off her phone so nobody could reconstruct her movements until she felt she was far enough from the scene of the crime. Then she called Ryan, who was getting worried, waiting for her. She told him she was lost in the desert and had left the cell phone at a gas station; she called Darryl, and even Travis, leaving messages on his cell. She played the part of the inconsolable friend. She wrote words of sympathy to the Alexander family, and sent a bunch of twenty irises to his mother, without realizing, through the irony of Fate, that in the language of flowers the iris symbolizes the triumph of the truth.

In 2015 Jodi Arias was sentenced to life in prison for premeditated murder.

The Dark Lady

Marissa Devault (United States)

The librarian glasses that Marissa Devault wanted to wear during her trial did not help clean up her image: she remained ambiguous and sinister. She wanted to pass as a victim, but she seemed, instead, more like a torturer. Her last name was also ambiguous, pronounced in two different ways, American and French, and she always laughed at the wrong moment. Only the hammer spoke clearly: it was that hammer that Marissa used to kill her husband Dale Harrell in his sleep, leaving it bloodstained at the scene of the crime.

On the night of January 14th, 2009, Dale Harrell, a man of thirty-four, was asleep in the bedroom of his home in Gilbert, a suburb of Phoenix, Arizona. At some point his wife, Marissa Devault, a thirty-two-year-old former stripper, came into the room and began to furiously hit her husband, again and again, in the head with a hammer. After reducing the man almost to a corpse, Marissa phoned the police. Seized by panic, on the spur of the moment she invented an attack by an unknown intruder. Then she confessed to having struck her husband in self-defense. According to Marissa, in fact, that night her husband had tried to rape and suffocate her. There was blood everywhere. It splattered red the walls, the lamps, the furniture. Clint Cobbett, one of the first policemen on the scene, found the woman in a "hysterical state on the verge of a hyperventilation attack" in front of the house, her clothes stained with blood. But he did not notice any sign of aggression, apart from a "slight reddening on the neck." In photos taken that night, there were no significant bruises, marks or scratches on Marissa's body. Even her nails were perfect, freshly manicured. The woman was arrested for aggravated assault and then released on bail. Dale Harrell, treated, but in serious condition, died on February 9th from a pulmonary embolism.

Various Versions

The version of the facts supplied by Marissa, once the intruder hypothesis was discarded, was therefore of homicide in self-defense. After her admission of guilt she said to the police: "I wanted him to know what I felt." She said that she'd shouted as she attacked him,

I am not one of your things!

She testified to years of abuse and treatment in the hospital as a result of the violence inflicted on her by Dale. However, none of the friends and relatives of the couple remembered episodes of the sort when questioned by the police. Later, Marissa told a different story, and tried to pin the murder on Stanley Cook, a friend af-

---

Marissa Devault's coming across as a reliable and fresh faced woman.

flicted with mental problems who had shared the house with the couple for a time. She even got him to sign a confession – but it was not accepted as valid by the authorities.

A strange incident took place in the last days of Harrell's throes of death. Marissa was found unconscious in a field not far from their home. She reported being attacked by a stranger while she was jogging. It was another lie. It emerged instead that, in need of money, she was trying to cash in on an insurance policy of $ 500.000 signed against the risk of an incapacitating injury to her spinal column. There was a part in this scheme, once again, for her accomplice-friend, Stanley Cook, who Marissa had asked to attack her such that she might be paralyzed. So the man struck her with a bat and took her a short distance away by car. He abandoned her along the side of the road. Stanley explained to the police that he also called Marissa on her cell phone, pretending to be worried by her silence, in an attempt to distance himself from the incident. The woman did not remain paralyzed, but the fake attack did supply the prosecution with important clues.

In January, 2009, Marissa Devault was charged with premeditated, first-degree murder. The State of Arizona announced its intention to ask for capital punishment for the severity of the crime: the culprit had brutally killed her husband for pecuniary gain. The defense responded with the syndrome of an abused woman and post-traumatic stress. The trial began five years later, in February, 2014, in the Maricopa County Court in Gilbert, Arizona.

A Family in Debt

When Marissa and Dale got married, on September 6th, 1999, she was already the mother of a child, Rhiannon, who Dale did not adopt. They then had two daughters together, Khiernan and Daihnnon. Only Rhiannon validated the hypothesis of domestic violence against her mother. During her testimony at the trial, she recalled many times when she and her sisters had barricaded themselves in their room, moving a chest of drawers against the door for fear that the violence of the arguing adults could spread to them.

She was asked by the defense counsel Andrew Clemency:

Have you ever seen your stepfather hit your mother?

"It happened often," said the girl, who was thirteen at the time of the murder. When the prosecuting attorney asked her if, vice versa, she had ever seen her mother hit her stepfather, Rhiannon replied: "She hit him, but not as much as he hit her."

In 2007, Marissa met Allen Flores through a website for "sugar daddies" looking for women "in need of affection." And money. She introduced Flores to her husband as the gay lover of her stepfather. Meanwhile, began a sexual relationship with him. Flores, in the two years of the relationship, lent Marissa $ 362.000; she agreed to pay him back by December 31st, 2009, signing two bank drafts dated 2007 and 2009. To reassure him, Marissa told Flores that she was waiting for a large inheritance, and had, in the meantime, taken out an insurance policy on her husband.

During the trial Flores said that he had strong fears about recovering his money, and admitted to having secretly gone through his lover's bank statements. Moreover, he said, Marissa had confided in him her plan to eliminate Dale. His testimony was crucial during the trial, but it was also called into serious doubt by Devault's defense. After the death of Dale Harrell, in fact, the police had examined the contents of Flores' computer and found child-pornographic material, a crime punishable by 20 years in prison. The man had been promised limited immunity in exchange for his testimony against Marissa Devault.

Another witness was called during the trial: Travis Tatro. Marissa met Tatro in 2000, when she worked in a nightclub as a stripper with the stage name Reesy Cup. They'd had a sexual relationship. Tatro said Devault had contacted him, and asked him "to take care" of her husband. Tatro, unsure of what the woman meant by this – either to teach the man a lesson, or to kill him – chose to ignore it.

The Psychiatric Examination

Doctor Janeen DeMarte, a psychologist who also testified in the case of Jodi Arias, was heard again during the Devault trial. The diagnosis was very clear: Marissa Devault was a psychopath. DeMarte described a disturbed and antisocial personality, and cited the excuses that the culprit had given to the family of her husband ("the family of Dale is in my heart . . . his mother and father have had to bear the worst loss in the world"), in contrast to the phone calls she'd made from the jail, where an "ironic attitude and lack of remorse emerged", almost making a mockery of the murder of her husband.

"The family of Dale Harrell waited for the remains of their son," the doctor testified, "which Devault would only release in exchange for the withdrawal of the legal case. It's a manipulative attitude that reflects an absence of repentance towards the family." While the clinical analysis of a defense psychologist, Dr. Jon Conte, emphasized the symptoms of physical and sexual abuse endured in childhood, DeMarte responded

They are both young women, with long dark hair and angelic faces, and both have been found guilty of having murdered their companions without remorse. Not only were the murderers Marissa Devault and Jodi Arias both originally from Arizona, both demonstrated a propensity to lie and present themselves as victims. Condemned to life in prison in the same courtroom one year apart, the two "dark ladies" now also share the same Maricopa County penitentiary.

with other contradictions: "Marissa Devault has described her mother and stepfather as violent towards her, but in the course of a telephone call from the jail, I heard her ask them to look after her children."

The Verdict

On April 30th, 2014, the jury condemned Marissa Devault to life in prison, saving her from capital punishment. On June 6th the sentence was confirmed, with the addition of no possibility of release on parole. Judge Roland Steinle, said of the culprit, in an uncommon statement of opinion: "She is a manipulator and she will continue to be one. She has her three daughters to thank for not being condemned to death. The circumstances of this crime have been horrible and, in my opinion, motivated by greed." Marissa Devault will never be released from prison.

The Ice Cream Murderess

Estibaliz Carranza (Austria)

A dark, mysterious and hidden place, like a cellar, is perfect for storing and forgetting things that have outlived their usefulness. Estibaliz Carranza, on the other hand, chose to use it to get rid of someone with certain defects of character, which, in her view, were no longer bearable.

E sti's eyes and ears are still full of the warm light of the Museumsquartier and the laughter of her friends. She warms up in her home after the bitter cold of a late November day. She has never liked the climate in Vienna, even though she has just spent a pleasant evening out. Or rather, she pretends that she has. She's still dressed, with Manfred already in bed. He hasn't said a word to her since they came back home. She can say now that the sham of the happy couple is over.

Esti sits down and waits. As soon as she hears his breathing become heavier, she slowly opens a drawer and takes out, just as carefully, a Beretta .22 caliber pistol, her most jealously kept secret and, above all others, her most loyal ally. She hides it behind her, advances along the side of the bed, points the barrel at the back of the man's head, and fires four shots. A large bloodstain expands over the sheets.

Then, from its hiding place, she takes out a chainsaw. She holds it tightly in both hands, just as they taught her in the course. She must cut the body into at least four pieces, even if the industrial

The icy beauty of Estibaliz Carranza during a judicial hearing.

freezer at her ice cream parlor is rather large. After putting nylon sheets up on the walls, to protect them from squirting blood, she chops up the body. She wraps what remains of the corpse in some sacks and takes them, two at a time, down to the cellar.

Afterward, in a big tub, she mixes cement, water, sand, and gravel. She submerges the severed limbs in the concrete. It will dry quickly and the great tub will become identical to the one next to it. The first time, for Holger, the operation was more complex and the result less perfect. In any case, she thought, no one is going to come snooping down here.

A Dangerous Place

Less than one year later, on June 10th, 2011, it was a couple of carpenters who made the terrible discovery. Restructuring work had just begun in the building when, in the cellar, they found four tubs full of hard concrete. Poking out of the tubs were human limbs: they recognized a head and a leg. Work stopped, and the police sequestered the whole building. Besides the tubs they discovered two rifles, a pistol, and a cell phone belonging to Manfred Hinterberger, a sales representative for ice cream machines and the son of a local politician. He had been missing since November of the previous year.

When the police interrogated the residents of the building on Oswaldgasse, the only one absent was Estibaliz Carranza; born in Mexico City of Spanish parents, she was the owner of the *Schleckeria* on the ground floor of the building. At the first sound of the siren, she had fled in a taxi, putting distance between herself and a place that was beginning to be – for her, this time – very dangerous.

Restlessness and Worry

The police issued an international arrest warrant and waited for the woman to come to the airport: there was a flight to Barcelona booked in her name. Esti, however, changed her plans. She had not completely decided on her destination, and asked the taxi driver to drive as far as possible. They went all the way to the Italian border and crossed it.

A woman like that can have all the men she wants. I only managed to look at her in the rearview mirror – but she was something, really sexy.

Mustafà Senel would later tell the police. The taxi driver was uneasy about the woman's charm, and her restlessness, so he tried to conclude the trip as soon as possible. He took her to a hotel in Cavazzo Carnico, between the highway and the mountains, and then drove off. The next day, Esti reached Udine. In the station she made friends with a young artist who, moved by her account of running away from a violent husband, let her stay at his place. He had the best of intentions. The woman's restless gaze, however, alerted the man: something was up. She was nervous. She repeatedly asked to consult the internet, once even asking for the young man's cellphone. Soon enough he thus ended up seeing story of the murders, the blood, the cellar. He notified the police, and Estibaliz's flight ended with an arrest by the Italian police.

Judgment Among Women

The trial took place very quickly. Estibaliz Carranza was charged with double murder, with having killed her ex-husband, Holger Holz (thirty years old), in 2008, and later a partner, Manfred

Hinterberger (forty-eight years old), in 2010. With the end of each love story, Esti put her man away in the cellar, as if he were a broken chair or an old bedside table.

There followed a few hearings, some psychiatric testimony, a full confession, and a sentence to life in prison, to be served in the Schwarzau criminal asylum. The jury was unanimous in finding her guilty. At the reading of the verdict, Esti wore a pearl-gray dress, close-fitting and elegant, which emphasized her youth. Her full lips were tightly pressed, her gaze unmoved, consistent with the nickname the papers had given her: "Eis Killer", the ice cream murderess.

> *It is rare that such heinous crimes are committed by a woman. But it is rarer still that the investigations of such cases are conducted by a woman prosecutor, Petra Freh, and that the spokesperson for the Court is a woman, Susanne Lehr, and that the psychiatrist tasked with investigating the recesses of the defendant's mind, Adelheid Kastner, is also a woman.*

The local newspaper, the *Messaggero Veneto*, made this comment, in reviewing this case that was of great interest to both the Italian and Austrian public and media.

MY TWO LIVES

In 2014, three years after in the verdict, Estibaliz Carranza published a book of memoirs, *My Two Lives*, written with the journalist Martina Prewein, in which she stated that she had repented of the crimes that she had committed. Since she became a mother in prison – she declares in the volume of more than 200 pages – she is able to understand what it may mean to lose a child, and in such an appalling way.

When she was arrested, on June 11th, 2011, Goidsargi Esti-baliz Carranza Zabala, not yet thirty-three years old, was expecting a baby from Roland, her new partner. She became a mother during her first months in prison. And she married Roland in prison. The child was entrusted to Carranza's mother. The psychiatrist who examined her was convinced that if she had not been stopped, she would have killed again.

CAPE TIMES ★

with BUSINESS REPORT   R7.00 incl VAT   Country R7.20 incl VAT   FRIDAY, FEBRUARY 15, 2013   25°C
See Page

Storm season
Get your Super Rugby
booklet today   **Inside**

Zero Dark Thirty
We review Kathryn Bigelow's film about the
assassination of Bin Laden   **Top of the Times**

ALL FROM GLORY: Oscar Pistorius (above) after winning a heat at the London Olympics, and in the right outside the Boschkop police station after being arrested for the murder of his girlfriend, Reeva Steenkamp (middle).   Pictures: CHRIS COLLINS

Screams, then gunshots

The Bullet
in the Chamber

Oscar Pistorius (South Africa)

On Valentine's Day, 2013, Oscar Pistorius kills his girlfriend, Reeva
Steenkamp. A successful actress and model, Steenkamp appears
on the covers of the most popular South African magazines. At the
crime scene: the weapon and the murderer. He is convicted, and
then, after only a year in prison, put under house arrest. But . . .

Fibular hemimelia: these terrible words accompanied the
birth of Oscar Pistorius, on November 22nd, 1986, in Johannesburg, South Africa. It meant that the newborn was born

without fibulae. This was terrible news for his mother, Sheila, and for those waiting for him outside the delivery room: his father, Henke, and little brother, Carl. Eleven months later, the doctors made their diagnosis: it was necessary to amputate both legs just under the knee. Shortly afterward, little Oscar learned to walk using prosthetic legs. Under these conditions, his life would not be normal. In fact, it wasn't, but not in ways one might expect. He was very good at sports, and succeeded in all kinds, from water polo to tennis. In 2003, he sustained a serious injury while playing the national sport, rugby, on the high school team. Another hard blow came a few months later, with the death of his mother. They were extremely close. She had always pushed him to fight back against adversity. For example, in the morning, before he went to school, she'd pack his lunch and write words of encouragement on the bag. It was during his long and complex rehabilitation from the rugby injury, however, that he discovered his true vocation, running. He had a verse from the Bible tattooed on his left shoulder. It began with the words:

Therefore I run, but not like one without an aim.

The Olympics

By twenty-one, Pistorius was a Paralympic champion in all the sprints: 100, 200 and 400 meters. He was encouraged by these results, and refused to compete only with physically disabled athletes. After a long debate (legal and scientific) with the IAAF, the international athletics federation, which claimed that the carbon fiber prosthesis Pistorius used would give him an advantage over normal athletes, he was finally allowed to take part in "normal" races.

The front page of the newspaper Cape Times *on the day of Oscar Pistorius' arrest.*

In 2011, at the World Championships, he won the silver medal in the 4x400 relay; the next year, in London, he was the first amputated athlete to take part in the Olympic Games, and he qualified for the semi-finals in the 400 meters race. Pistorius turned his disability into a strength, a particularity to show off with pride: nicknamed "Blade Runner", he appeared in advertising posters in the most diverse poses, all designed deliberately to emphasize . . . what was not there. A media personality, he signed million-dollar contracts with the various sponsors, including the sportswear giant Nike, which coined the slogan "I am the Bullet in the Chamber", referring to the explosiveness of his burst from the blocks. These words were sadly prophetic.

Death Behind the Door

On the morning of February 14th, 2013, Pistorius, who is in bed in his home in Pretoria, hears noises coming from the bathroom. He thinks that it is a burglar who has broken into his home.

South Africa the problem of security is deeply felt, as petty crime is particularly widespread; in a short time he'll move to Johannesburg, which is a relief because the house he just bought is equipped with an advanced security system. But at that moment he panics: he takes his Brazilian-made .9mm Parabellum pistol, which he keeps hidden under the bedside table, and fires four shots through the locked bathroom door. However, when he realizes that on the other side of the door there lies the lifeless body of his partner Reeva, who he thought had been in bed, he is desperate and bursts into tears. This is his version of the events.

Manslaughter or Murder?

The trial – during which Pistorius never denied having fired the shots – began a year later (in the meantime, the accused was released on bail) with a psychiatric report to evaluate whether the accused was able to understand the consequences of his actions. He was diagnosed with a generalized anxiety disorder, which characterized him as a "mistrustful and suspicious person, obsessed with security." In any case, the trial would go forward. There was no jury (which was abolished in the apartheid years), only one judge, Thokozile Masipa, who was assisted by two consultants, seated diligently beside her.

In court, the prosecution maintained that things did not go as the defendant claimed: in its view, after a furious argument between the couple (which might have occurred on the balcony of the home), a frightened Reeva had locked herself in the bathroom, where she was then struck by three of the four bullets fired through the door. Pistorius had deliberately intended to kill the person in the bathroom, whoever it was, and it was important to stress the intentionality of the act. The prosecutor's words were very clear:

Pistorius acted to kill, recklessly and with an excessive use of force.

Many, too Many, Elements do not Add Up . . .

So – replied the defense – if the murder was premeditated, why wasn't Pistorius wearing his prostheses, a fact confirmed by ballistic evidence? He did not even have them when he broke down the bathroom door with a cricket bat, which was later found with traces of blood in the bedroom. A witness said he first heard shots, then screams – female – followed by more shots: he was about 330 yards from the crime scene. Another witness, on the other hand, stated that he had heard desperate crying, and a voice – male – asking, three times, for help. The investigators also sifted through the messages that the couple had sent each other on their Smartphones. While there was nothing remarkable about 90% of them, Reeva reproved him several times for being jealous and possessive. In one, from three weeks before her death, she wrote:

Sometimes the way you verbally attack me frightens me.

However, on the Valentine's card she had bought him, which Pistorius himself read in court, she had written: "Today is the best day to tell you I love you."

Some cracks in the prosecution's case remained: an acoustic engineer maintained it was very unlikely that Steenkamp's screams – from the bathroom, with the door locked – could have been heard hundreds of yards away, or that, from the same distance, one could to distinguish male from female screams. And then, numerous experts and witnesses supported the claim that Pistorius was truly shaken and desperate in the moments after the murder: one of his neighbors, who rushed in, said he saw Pistorius praying over his partner's lifeless body, while repeating:

I shot her. I thought she was a burglar. I shot her.

On October 21st, 2014, Pistorius was found guilty of manslaughter, which according to the South African penal code is the killing of a human being through negligent behavior. He was sentenced to 5 years in prison, to be served at the Kgosi Mampuru II Correctional Centre in Pretoria.

Judge Masipa, who during the trial had received threats and had been put under armed escort, thus believed the defense. While it emerged that Pistorius possessed a turbulent personality which often led him to unexpected outbursts of anger, and that he loved weapons excessively, these remained side issues. To most people, it seemed that the punishment was surprisingly mild. Reeva's mother stated to journalists there she was sure that sooner or later Pistorius would kill again. But the evidence to prove the voluntary nature or premeditation of the crime was confused and insufficient. The prosecutor unequivocally chastised the court about the sentence:

It is a scandalously light sentence devoid of any logic, which no court with good sense would ever have passed!

Index

283

Geographical Index

Photo Credits